Churchill and the Avoidable War
Could World War II have been Prevented?

Dedicated to the Memory of
The Rt Hon Sir Martin Gilbert CBE
Teacher, Counsellor, Friend
Ich hatte einen Kameraden...

*"There never was a war in all history easier to prevent
by timely action than the one which has just desolated such great
areas of the globe. It could have been
prevented in my belief without the firing of a single shot...but no
one would listen and one by one
we were all sucked into the awful whirlpool."*
—Winston S. Churchill, *Fulton, Missouri, 5 March 1946*

...And in memory of
The Rt Hon Sir Winston Leonard Spencer Churchill
KG OM CH TD FRS

*"One who never turned his back
but marched breast forward,
Never doubted clouds would break,
Never dreamed, though right were worsted,
Wrong would triumph,
Held we fall to rise,
Are baffled to fight better,
Sleep to wake."*

Churchill and the Avoidable War
Could World War II
have been Prevented?

by Richard M. Langworth

DRAGONWYCK
PUBLISHING

1 3 5 7 9 10 8 6 4 2

First edition, 2015
Dragonwyck Publishing Inc.,
Moultonborough, New Hampshire USA
Also published as a Kindle Single®

Cover design by Richard Boxhall

ISBN-13: 978-1518690358
ISBN-10: 1518690351

Table of Contents

Preface

Germany Disarmed

"After the end of the World War of 1914 there was a deep conviction and almost universal hope that peace would reign in the world. ... The phrase 'the war to end war,' was on every lip, and measures had been taken to turn it into reality. ... Instead, a gaping void was opened in the national life of the German people ... and into that void after a pause there strode a maniac of ferocious genius, the repository and expression of the most virulent hatreds that have ever corroded the human breast—Corporal Hitler."

—Churchill, *The Gathering Storm*, 1948

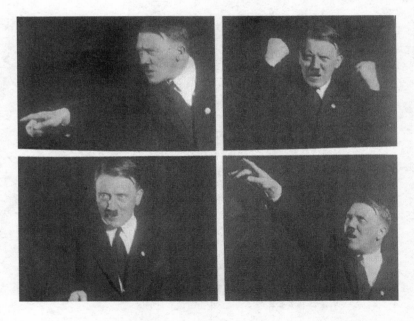

The Corporal turned Führer, 1934. (Bundesarchhiv Bild 102-10460)

World War II was the defining event of our age—the climactic clash between democracy and tyranny, liberty and slavery. It killed more people than any war in history. It led to revolutions, religious and sectarian strife, the demise of empires, a protracted Cold War not resolved for half a century—and perhaps still not resolved. Its aftershocks abide in the Middle East and Asia, attitudes toward foreign involvement by the United States, a Europe at once united and disunited. It was the war that made us what we are today. Yet Winston Churchill maintained that it all could have been prevented.

This book examines Churchill's argument: his prescriptions to prevent war, not in retrospect but at the time—his formulas, his actions, the degree to which he pursued them. We must bear in mind that Churchill was out of office, that he had no plenary authority. But he did have stature, and the challenges were great: the rise of Hitler; the rearming of Germany; violations of the Versailles treaty; the push for German hegemony, the remilitarization of the Rhineland, the *Anschluss* with Austria, the seizure of Czechoslovakia; missed opportunities for useful relationships with Russia and America. Of course these challenges were not to Britain alone—particularly in the cases of the Rhineland and Czechoslovakia.

The result is a kind of "re-revisionism": a corrective to traditional arguments about the inevitability of war once Hitler came to power, by Churchill's critics, and by defenders who insist no one listened to him. It is based not on hindsight but on what really happened—evidence that has been "hiding in public" for many years.

To examine Churchill's proposals at the time might suggest that we should not quote Churchill's memoir, *The Second World War,* since it was written, as he described it, "in the after-light." Not entirely. As Churchill wrote in his preface to that work: "I have adhered to my rule of never criticising any measure of war or policy after the event unless I had before expressed publicly or formally my opinion or warning about it." Accordingly, I refer to *The Gathering Storm*—the first volume, which chiefly concerns us here—when it reflects what Churchill said and did *at the time*, or when he simply recounts facts.

We must not be, as a wise colleague warned me, "innocent readers of *The Gathering Storm*." His book was not history, Churchill said. It was a defence of his beliefs and actions. Lord Tedder in his memoirs, *With Prejudice,* cites a supposed exchange between Churchill and his friend Jan Smuts, who allegedly says: "You…could have written the true history of the war, and instead of that you have produced these books." Churchill replies: "These are *my* story. If someone else likes to write *his* story, let him." My concluding chapter offers an example relating to Prime Minister Baldwin, on which many have concluded Churchill was unduly censorious.

This book makes no attempt to pillory Churchill's predecessors as prime minister. To that end, the word "appeasement" appears nowhere in this text. I emphasize this bearing in mind Churchill's final words in Parliament about his predecessor: "Whatever else history may or may not say about these terrible, tremendous years, we can be sure that Neville Chamberlain acted with perfect sincerity according to his lights and strove to the utmost of his capacity and authority, which were powerful, to save the world from the awful, devastating struggle."

To her father's admirers the late Lady Soames would always offer a commandment: "Thou shalt not say what my father would do today." Modern situations are vastly different. The threat today is diffuse; even in its totality it is by no means comparable to that embodied by

8

Nazi Germany. Was Churchill right that World War II was preventable? The answer, I think, is yes—at one juncture in particular—but with great difficulty. Was he right that it is foolish to put off unpleasant reality "until self-preservation strikes its jarring gong"? Undoubtedly. The problem for leaders today is to judge when discretion should take priority over action, when diplomacy is a feasible option, when and where to deploy a bluff, and when, sometimes, to let an opponent think you are just a little crazy.

It is proper to consider the lessons of the past as a guide to similar challenges now and in the future. But as Churchill wrote, "Let no one look down on those honourable, well-meaning men whose actions are chronicled in these pages, without searching his own heart, reviewing his own discharge of public duty, and applying the lessons of the past to his future conduct." We must avoid applying the fatal decisions in *Churchill's Lost Years* to today's problems—yet that is what the Churchillian critique of the 1930s has been used for, from the 1948 Berlin blockade through the Cold War, the Korean and Vietnam wars, the Suez and Cuban crises, Saddam Hussein's Iraq, North Korea and Iran.

The 75th anniversary of Munich in 2013 was accompanied by analogies. During the uproar over Syria's chemical weapons, the American Secretary of State declared, "This is our Munich moment." Later his opponents labelled the easing of sanctions on Iran as "another Munich." All these comparisons are inapt, except as examples of that lack of resolve which is part of human nature. The Germany of 1938 was both a greater threat and less suicidal than today's enemies. The situations are not the same.

"History doesn't repeat," Mark Twain said, "but it does rhyme." If there are echoes today to the challenges of Germany and the Rhineland, of Austria and Munich, we should consider what we can learn in terms of human nature, rather than equating them with modern conditions. Churchill called his memoirs "a contribution to history." Let us consider what history can contribute to our thinking today, and thus derive wisdom from it.

I should like to thank my wife Barbara, as ever my tireless proof-reader and adviser, along with several generous colleagues. Professor Warren F. Kimball of Rutgers University, President Larry Arnn of Hillsdale College, and historian Andrew Roberts thoroughly vetted my manuscript and cited numerous points in need of improvement, including places where I should make a better argument or use a better quote. I also thank Gordon Wise of Curtis Brown, agents for the Churchill Literary Estate. Particularly they held my nose to my own grindstone, pointing to every violation of my goal to dwell only on Churchill's actions at the time of these events, not his impressions in hindsight. Professors Paul Addison and David Dilks were of immeasurable assistance in reading parts of this book and reminding me never to accept Churchill's evaluations of the problems without verifying his contentions and opposing points of view based on the facts as they existed. This does not imply that my colleagues endorse all the conclusions, which are mine alone.

—Richard M. Langworth
Eleuthera, Bahamas, 25 March 2015

Chapter 1

Germany Arming:
Encounters with Hitler, 1930-1934

"I do not suppose there has ever been such a pacifist-minded Government. There is the Prime Minister [Ramsay MacDonald] who in the war proved in the most extreme manner and with very great courage his convictions and the sacrifices he would make for what he believed was the cause of pacifism. The Lord President of the Council [Stanley Baldwin] is chiefly associated in the public mind with the repetition of the prayer, 'Give peace in our time.'"
—Churchill, House of Commons, 30 July 1934

Churchill reading at his stand-up desk, Chartwell, 1930s. (Wikimedia)

There is no evidence that Churchill read *Mein Kampf* until 1933,[1] but he was aware of Hitler earlier. His friend General Sir Ian Hamilton furnished the first reference to Hitler in Churchill's official biography, in reporting the views of the German shipping magnate and onetime Chancellor Wilhelm Cuno in October 1930.[2]

What Hamilton described as Hitler's "scoop" in the 1930 German elections was, according to Cuno, natural and hopeful: "The whole question…was whether the change would be to the right or to the left…They had got their swing to the right and he hoped that responsibility of power would make this new Government more moderate in action than it had been in words."[3]

There is no record of a reply, but Churchill was certainly paying attention, particularly, at that time, to war debt payments. The Lausanne Conference (June-July 1932) had ended payments of German reparations, but not Britain's or France's war debt to the United States. To Churchill, the agreement was therefore incomplete:

Of course, anything which removes friction between Germany and France is to the good. [But] within less than fifteen years of the Great War Germany has been virtually freed from all burden of repairing the awful injuries which she wrought upon her neighbours. True, there are 3,000,000,000 marks which are to be payable by Germany, but I notice that Herr Hitler, who is the moving impulse behind the German Government and may be more than that very soon, took occasion to state yesterday that within a few months that amount would not be worth three marks. That is an appalling statement to be made while the ink is yet damp upon the parchment of the Treaty. Therefore I say that Germany has been virtually freed from all reparations.[4]

This was Churchill's first reference to Hitler in Parliament. What, he asked, had become of "the Carthaginian peace of which we used to hear so much? That has gone….It is Germany that has received an infusion of blood from the nations with whom she went to war and by whom she was decisively defeated."[5]

Hitler's and Churchill's Near-Meeting

Remarkably, Hitler and Churchill almost met, in Munich, on 30 August 1932.

Churchill had travelled to the Continent to tour Danubian battlefields of the First Duke of Marlborough, whose biography he was writing. En route, he later wrote, "I drove into Munich, and spent the best part of a week there. At the Regina Hotel a gentleman introduced himself to some of my party [who] spoke a great deal about 'the Führer,' with whom he appeared to be intimate."[6]

The gentleman was Ernst "Putzi" Hanfstaengl, who wrote in his memoirs: "I landed with Hitler at Munich airport to find a telephone message awaiting me from my acquaintance, Randolph Churchill. His family were staying with a party at the Hotel Continental (not the Regina Palace, Sir Winston's memory plays him false), wanted me to join them for dinner, and hoped that I would able to bring Hitler along." Hanfstaengl duly invited Hitler, who was reluctant: "What on earth would I talk to him about?," the Führer reportedly said.

In the restaurant, Hanfstaengl joined Churchill, Randolph, their daughter Sarah and Winston's friend and scientific adviser Frederick Lindemann. It was here that Churchill made the now-famous remark: "Tell your boss from me that anti-Semitism may be a good starter, but it is a bad sticker."[7]

Excited at the prospect of a meeting, Hanfstaengl excused himself and went in search of his boss, whom he found near his apartment. "Herr Hitler," he said, "don't you realise the Churchills are sitting in the restaurant?...They are expecting you for coffee and will think this a deliberate insult.'" Hitler said he was unshaven and had too much to do. The plan fizzled.

Hanfstaengl records another Churchill remark at that Munich dinner: "How does your chief feel about an alliance between your country, France and England?" Hanfstaengl was "transfixed." Churchill's remark, if he said it, suggests that he hoped to prevent another war by diplomacy that might address Germany's grievances over the Versailles Treaty. This would have been very much in character. As Churchill said years later, "Meeting jaw to jaw is better than war."[8]

The Harvard-educated Hanfstaengl is generally thought reliable. As Hitler's representative to the overseas press, he tried to exert a moderating influence, but fell out of favour with the Nazi hierarchy in 1936. Suspecting he was marked for assassination by Goebbels, he hastily left Germany in 1937, and wound up in England, where he was imprisoned as an enemy alien. A Canadian prison camp handed him over to the United States in 1942, he advised President Roosevelt on the Nazis and their leader.

"Thus Hitler lost his only chance of meeting me," Churchill cutely put it. "Later on, when he was all-powerful, I was to receive several invitations from him. But by that time a lot had happened, and I excused myself."[9]

Germany's Military Surge

In mid-1932 Chancellor Franz von Papen[10] demanded that Germany be allowed to rearm. British Foreign Secretary Sir John Simon replied firmly that this was proscribed by the Versailles Treaty. Churchill said Simon had "done more to consolidate peace in Europe than any words spoken on behalf of Great Britain for some years."[11] But Simon's firm line would not last long, and Hitler would prove far more determined than Papen.

After the July 1932 election, the Nazis, now the Reichstag's largest party, forced a vote of no confidence and another election in November. They lost seats in that election, but after various attempts to form coalitions failed, Papen advised President Hindenburg to send for Hitler, who became chancellor on 30 January 1933. Papen became vice-chancellor, but by mid-1934 he resigned; a few weeks later Hindenburg died, and the last right-wing opposition to Hitler vanished.

Less than three months later, Churchill issued his first warning about the Hitler regime. After the Great War, he said, the world had been told...

...that Germany would be a democracy with Parliamentary institutions. All that has been swept away. You have dictatorship—most grim dictatorship. You have militarism and appeals to every form of fighting spirit....You have these martial or pugnacious manifestations, and also this persecution of the Jews....I cannot help rejoicing that the Germans have not got the heavy cannon, the thousands of military aeroplanes and the tanks of various sizes for which they have been pressing in order that their status may be equal to that of other countries.[12]

This was not the time, Churchill added, to pursue disarmament—especially the current proposal that France reduce her army from 700,000 to 400,000. France, he added, "still has memories."[13]

15

The Failure of Disarmament

In those days there was no shortage of treaties and disarmament conferences. In 1921, the Washington Naval Treaty had set a strength ratio for capital ships of approximately 5:5:3:1.75:1.75 between Britain, the United States, Japan, Italy, and France. In the same year the Mixed Commission on Armaments sought to ban chemical warfare and strategic bombing; this was vetoed by Britain, which feared it would limit the ability to control its empire. The Kellogg-Briand Pact (1925, with 65 signatories) denounced wars of aggression but set no guidelines for responding to them. The same year, seven Locarno Treaties settled post-World War I borders. Ominously, while guaranteeing western borders, Locarno left those of Germany and Poland "open to revision."

The ongoing Geneva Conference (1932-37) began with Papen's demands for lifting the armaments limits imposed at Versailles—but the French would not agree without security commitments from Britain and the United States, which were not forthcoming. Hitler took Germany out of the Geneva talks in 1933.

More proposals occurred in 1934. In January, Churchill reacted to a British White Paper advocating further disarmament to achieve better relations with Hitler in prescient tones that predicted the future Blitz of London:

...I cannot see in the present administration of Germany any assurance that they would be more nice-minded in dealing with a vital and supreme situation than was the Imperial Government of Germany...[We may] be confronted on some occasion with a visit from an

ambassador, and may have to give an answer in a very few hours; and if that answer is not satisfactory, within the next few hours the crash of bombs exploding in London and cataracts of masonry and fire and smoke will apprise us of any inadequacy which has been permitted in our aerial defences....[14]

In February 1934 Hitler agreed with Poland to renounce for ten years all claims to the Polish Corridor, created at Versailles to give the newly constructed Polish republic an outlet to the sea. Hailed as a sign of Hitler's restraint, this promise would vanish long before ten years.

Also in February, Parliament rejected a proposal, initiated at Geneva by Prime Minister Ramsay MacDonald, for equilibrium in armaments between the great powers, which would have given Germany everything it wanted. Almost alone among leading figures, Churchill rejoiced in the no vote: "False ideas have been spread about the country that disarmament means peace....The Romans had a maxim: 'Shorten your weapons and lengthen your frontiers.' But our maxim seems to be: 'Diminish your weapons and increase your obligations.' Aye, and 'diminish the weapons of our friends.'"[15]

Of course, it has been argued, the British government was aware of the dangers, but labouring under economic and financial constraints. Churchill knew of these constraints, and spoke of them often. Preparation may be expensive, but not as expensive as war.

That same February 1934, the Cabinet's Defence Requirements Committee ruled that henceforth defence policy would assume that Germany, not Japan, was Britain's principal long-term enemy, and recommended a five-year programme of rearmament. This largely vindicated Churchill; but proclaiming the right policy does not automatically assure it.

In July 1934, France proposed an "Eastern Locarno," to finalize the borders of Germany, Russia, Poland, Czechoslovakia, Estonia, Latvia and Lithuania. This had the irony of naming both future aggressors (Germany and Russia) and future victims (the Czechs, Poles, Latvians, Lithuanians and Estonians). It came to nothing, and did not advance prospects of peace. Churchill declared:

When you have peace you will have disarmament, but there has been during these years a steady deterioration in the relations between different countries and a rapid increase in armaments that has gone on in spite of the endless flow of oratory, of well meaning sentiments, of perorations, and of banquets. Europe will be secure when nations no longer feel themselves in danger as many of them do now....I could not see how better you can prevent war than by confronting an aggressor with the prospect of such a vast concentration of force, moral and material, that even the most reckless, even the most infuriated leader, would not attempt to challenge those great forces.[16]

At the outbreak of World War I, Churchill recalled, "we had a supreme fleet; nobody could get at us in this island; and we had powerful friends on the continent of Europe, who were likely to be involved in any quarrel before we were. But today, with our aviation in its present condition, we are in a far worse position."[17] As Chancellor of the Exchequer in 1925-29, Churchill had followed government priorities that restricted defence spending;

from the advent of Hitler, he consistently favoured all
necessary measures to rearm, with priority to the air force.

"The Causes of War"

Churchill's views in these early skirmishes over
Germany were encapsulated during a radio broadcast,
"The Causes of War," delivered 16 November 1934.
Britain, he warned, was "in mortal danger." Disarmament
hadn't worked, nor was disarmament alone enough:
"We must remove grievances and injustice," he
said. "Let moral disarmament come and physical
disarmament will soon follow." But there was at present
no such possibility. All the nations of Europe faced was
"the old grim choice our forebears had to face, namely,
whether we shall submit to the will of a stronger nation or
whether we shall prepare to defend our rights, our liberties
and indeed our lives."[18]
A week later, in the Commons, Churchill delivered a
powerful rebuke to the forces of dither and timidity:

*What is the great new fact which has broken in upon us
during the last eighteen months? Germany is rearming....
Never in our history have we been in a position where we
could be liable to be blackmailed, or forced to surrender
our possessions, or take some action which the wisdom of
the country or its conscience would not allow.*[19]

As was his practice, Churchill sent an advance text
of "The Causes of War" to the Foreign Office for review.
He received a prescient reply from an assistant under-
secretary, Orme Sargent.[20] While discounting the idea that

Hitler wanted immediate war, Sargent believed the German Chancellor was...

... hoping to play off one Power against the other—Great Britain against France, Italy against France, Poland against Czechoslovakia, Russia against Japan, etc.—and then using the threat of force against each Power when it is isolated. Great Britain would probably be the last Power to be dealt with but its turn will come. The chief cause of war in such conditions is the feeling among the other nations that in a struggle with Germany they will not be able to count upon their neighbours; and in the eyes of Europe the chief neighbour—the neighbour who really counts—is Great Britain. How far can Europe rely on Great Britain when it is continually hearing the voices of the pacifists and isolationists drowning that of the Government?[21]

Sargent's appraisal was as accurate as anyone's, including Churchill's. Over the ensuing years, cleverly orchestrated by Hitler, the western democracies would meet most of his objectives possible without war—until 1939, when Germany would spring forward, armed to the teeth.

Chapter 2

Germany Armed:
"Hitler and His Choice" 1935-36

"Recently he has offered many words of reassurance, eagerly lapped up by those who have been so tragically wrong about Germany in the past. Only time can show, but, meanwhile, the great wheels revolve; the rifles, the cannon, the tanks, the shot and shell, the air-bombs, the poison-gas cylinders, the aeroplanes, the submarines, and now the beginnings of a fleet, flow in ever-broadening streams from the already largely war-mobilised arsenals and factories of Germany." —Churchill, November 1935

"Number Juggler Churchill and the German Aircraft": Churchill warns of German rearmament from a box labelled "Spitzel-breichte" (Spy reports). Olaf Gulbransson in Die Brennessel (The Nettle), *Munich, 18 December 1934.*

C hurchill's critics have used his writings to argue that he was "for Hitler before he was against him." As a politician Churchill did appreciate Hitler's skill and nerve. With his innate optimism he even hoped, in one or two articles, that Hitler might mellow. But in his fundamental understanding Churchill never wavered. He was right all along: dead right.

A problem in warning of the Nazi danger was Britain's preoccupation with Depression at home, and the Labour government's failure to cope. In mid-1931 Labour Prime Minister Ramsay MacDonald formed a national government with the Conservatives and Liberals. In a November election, "national" candidates won an overwhelming 554 seats, but most of them were Conservatives.

MacDonald was angrily expelled from his shattered Labour Party. Despondent and ill, he resigned the premiership on 7 June 1935, in favour of the Conservative leader, Stanley Baldwin. The switch embodied no change in outlook toward Germany, although under both MacDonald and Baldwin, modest defence increases had begun.

Sombre Forebodings

Churchill had served Baldwin's 1924-29 Conservative government as Chancellor of the Exchequer, but had fallen out with the Tories afterward, when his principled resistance over self-government for India effectively barred him from their inner councils. It is often argued that he would have been more effective over Germany had he been less defiant over India. But to Churchill, the government was making the same mistake in both cases: retrenching to avoid asking things of the people that, they feared, the people would not give.

"The German situation is increasingly sombre," Churchill wrote his wife in March 1935.[22] When Parliament voted a modest increase of £10 million in armaments, an enraged Hitler had refused to receive British Foreign Secretary John Simon[23]—"a measure," Churchill wrote, "of the conviction which Hitler has of the German Air Force and Army....it is very difficult to know exactly what they have prepared, but that danger gathers apace is indisputable."

Churchill was by now receiving detailed information on German armament. "Enormous sums of money are being spent on German aviation and upon other armaments," he told the Commons in March. "I wish we could get at the figures....I believe they would stagger us."[24]

"Although the House listened to me with close attention," Churchill recalled later, "I felt a sensation of despair. To be so entirely convinced and vindicated in a matter of life and death to one's country, and not to be able to make Parliament and the nation heed the warning, or bow to the proof by taking action, was an experience most painful."[25]

The government maintained that Britain had not lost air superiority. This is not the place for lengthy comparisons, which have been exhaustively documented elsewhere. Some of the figures Churchill cited proved later to be exaggerations; his alarm, however, was justified. Germany was fast catching up, particularly in the air. As early as February 1935, for example, Britain's Air Ministry had estimated 850 German first-line and reserve aircraft, against the most optimistic figure of 453 for Britain.[26]

On March 25th, Hitler announced German "parity" with Britain in air power. Churchill saw the politics of this, calling it a "sensation" which "stultifies everything that Baldwin has said and incidentally vindicates all the assertions that I have made."[27]

Hitler as Peacemaker

On 3 May 1935 Hitler wrote a revealing letter to Lord Rothermere,[28] one of his British admirers, appealing for Anglo-German understanding. He had worked for rapport with "England" for fifteen years, Hitler said. Together, Britain and Germany might ensure peace for a generation. Except for his references to Aryan supremacy, a reader might think his letter was written by the Pope.

Britain like Germany, Hitler wrote, had gained nothing by the last war, which had "swept away the pick of their manhood." Until 1914, the "two Germanic peoples" had spent 500 years without conflict: Britain had "opened a great part of the world to the white race." Germany's "cultural and economic activities for the welfare and the greatness of this old Continent are difficult to estimate." Their mutual enemy now was Bolshevism, which "tears away a mighty slice of European-Asiatic breathing-space" ['Lebensraum'] from "the only possible international world economy." As a result the British Empire was "weakened rather than strengthened."

Hitler then spoke of his desire for peace: "For fifteen years I have been scorned and ridiculed…by the petty politicians, who possessed no understanding." In the course of 4000 to 5000 speeches, not once had he regarded the late war as anything "but a desperate, Niebelung-like war of annihilation, rising to frenzy, between the Germanic peoples.…I have preached unswervingly the necessity of both nations burying the hatchet forever."

He was an honourable man, Hitler insisted, and such an understanding "cannot be made without honour." He had "derived from Fate the heavy task of giving back again to a great people and state by every means its natural honour." But never had he vacillated or strayed from his desire for peace:

Herein resides perhaps the faith—exaggerated, as many believe—in my own personality. I believe, my dear Lord Rothermere, [in restoring] a good and enduring understanding between both great Germanic peoples.....There is in Germany a fine saying: that the Gods love and bless him who seems to demand the impossible. I want to believe in this Divinity!

Hitler in this letter seems to agree with Churchill about the numerous post-war treaties: "All the so-called mutual-assistance pacts which are being hatched today will subserve discord rather than peace." Only Anglo-German understanding would provide "a force for peace and reason of 120 million people of the highest type." It would combine "the unique colonial ability and sea-power of England" with "one of the greatest soldier-races of the world....Were this understanding extended by the joining up of the American nation, then it would, indeed, be hard to see who in the world could disturb peace without willfully and consciously neglecting the interests of the White race."[29]

Churchill's reply to Rothermere, invoking his broad knowledge of history, cut through Hitler's arguments in a paragraph:

If his proposal means that we should come to an understanding with Germany to dominate Europe I think this would be contrary to the whole of our history. We have on all occasions been the friend of the second strongest power in Europe and have never yielded ourselves to the strongest power. You know the old fable of the jackal who went hunting with the tiger and what happened after the hunt was over. Thus Elizabeth resisted Philip II of Spain. Thus William III and Marlborough resisted Louis XIV. Thus Pitt resisted Napoleon, and thus we all resisted William II of Germany. Only by taking this path and effort have we preserved ourselves and our liberties, and reached our present position. I see no reason myself to change from this traditional view.

Anglo-German understanding would be agreeable, Churchill added, "provided they included France and gave fair consideration to Italy. Perhaps you will consider this."[30]

Rothermere did not accept Churchill's suggestion. He did not trust Hitler, he replied, but Britain was defenceless, France undone by socialism and communism, Italy preoccupied with its invasion of Abyssinia: "Once Hitler feels strong enough, I believe he will challenge all three Powers, and from what one knows of their respective armaments Hitler will have an easy win....Unless we can steer clear some way or another, the blow, in my opinion, will inevitably fall before the end of next year."[31] He was right about the blow.

Nursing a persistent delusion, Lord Rothermere would continue to plead for accommodations with Hitler as late as 1939. Hitler, he told Churchill in 1935, "has a strange sentimental regard for me. I think I told you, he offered to give me one of the very latest German planes, but I refused."[32] Solemn vows of friendship and generosity were characteristic of Hitler. They often hid sinister purposes.

"Hitler and His Choice"

In the same week of his exchange with Rothermere, Churchill was asked by *The Strand* magazine to write about Hitler. "I should like you to be as outspoken as you possibly can," wrote editor Reeves Shaw, "and absolutely frank in your judgment of his methods."[33]

Churchill's November 1935 article, "The Truth About Hitler," had a long life. Two years later, Churchill published a revision, "Hitler and His Choice," in *Great Contemporaries*, his book of character sketches.[34] Reviewing the draft, the Foreign Office thought it harsh.[35] Churchill toned it down, but they still didn't like it. Yet "Hitler and His Choice" has been quoted ever since to suggest that Churchill was once pro-Hitler.

Similar in tone was Churchill's article, "This Age of Government by Great Dictators," published in the *News of the World* the week after release of *Great Contemporaries*. Most of this was from "Hitler and His Choice," but Churchill—perhaps vexed at the Foreign Office's read on his book chapter—redeployed two sentences from his 1935 *Strand* article:

"It is on this mystery of the future that history will pronounce Hitler either a monster or a hero. It is this which will determine whether he will rank in Valhalla with Pericles, with Augustus and with Washington, or welter in the inferno of human scorn with Attila and Tamerlane."[36]

None of this materially changes Churchill's doubts about Hitler. Ah, say the critics, but what about this, from yet another article in September 1937:

One may dislike Hitler's system and yet admire his patriotic achievement. If our country were defeated, I hope

27

we should find a champion as indomitable to restore our courage and lead us back to our place among the nations. I have on more than one occasion made my appeal in public that the Führer of Germany should now become the Hitler of peace....success should bring a mellow, genial air and, by altering the mood to suit the new circumstances, preserve and consolidate in tolerance and goodwill what has been gained by conflict.[37]

Again, Churchill here was merely expressing what Hitler *should* do, allowing for the possibility that Hitler would mellow. He was no enemy of Germany, but it was his duty to warn Britain: "I can quite understand that this action of mine would not be popular in Germany. Indeed, it was not popular anywhere."[38] But Churchill was never a poll-watcher. He said, not what he thought the people wanted to hear, but what they *should* hear:

You cannot expect English people to be attracted by the brutal intolerances of Nazidom, though these may fade with time. On the other hand, we all wish to live on friendly terms with Germany. We know that the best Germans are ashamed of the Nazi excesses, and recoil from the paganism on which they are based. We certainly do not wish to pursue a policy inimical to the legitimate interests of Germany, but [we cannot] agree to their having a free hand so far as we are concerned in Central and Southern Europe. This means that they would devour Austria and Czechoslovakia as a preliminary to making a gigantic middle-Europe bloc. It would certainly not be in our interest to connive at such policies of aggression.[39]

Today, knowing precisely what Hitler was, it is possible to scoff at Churchill for tempering his writings in 1935-37, urged by the Foreign Office, or his own characteristic optimism. Yet Churchill had told "The Truth About Hitler" from the start. As Martin Gilbert wrote: "...neither the toned-down essay [in *Great Contemporaries*] nor the conciliatory article in the *Evening Standard* marked any change in Churchill's attitude...."[40]

The Anglo-German Naval Agreement

Suggesting perhaps the confusion of counsel in high British circles, the Anglo-German Naval Agreement of 18 June 1935 set German navy tonnage at 35% of the Royal Navy's, much larger than allowed by the Versailles Treaty. Signed without French approval, it was hotly debated in the Commons. The National government was accused of hypocrisy, claiming to stand with Versailles and the League of Nations while making its own deals with Germany. A further complication was the League demand for sanctions against Italy for its invasion of Abyssinia, a side issue, thought Churchill, that could alienate Italy at the wrong time. (For further discussion of this aspect, see Chapter 8.)

Churchill was silent on the Naval Agreement until July 11th. Some have contended that he supported it, using a partial quote: "We have made a separate agreement for ourselves, of a perfectly innocent character..." In the round, however, his speech hardly minced words. The Agreement, he said,

...made it very difficult for us to remonstrate too strongly with Italy without being exposed to the somewhat severe reply that when we think our particular interests are involved we show but little consideration....the League of Nations has been weakened by our action, the principle of collective security has been impaired....British influence has to some extent been dissipated, and our moral position, or at any rate our logical position, has been to some extent obscured. You could not have had a more complete and perfect example of how not to do it....In the name of what is called practical realism, we have seemed to depart from the principle of collective security in a very notable fashion.[41]

On July 22nd, he again emphasised his regrets: "I do not believe for a moment that this isolated action by Great Britain will be found to work for the cause of peace. The immediate reaction is that every day the German Fleet approaches a tonnage which gives it absolute command of the Baltic, and very soon one of the deterrents of a European war will gradually fade away." [42]

Despite this, Churchill voted with the government, and has been accused of misleading readers of *The Gathering Storm* by implying greater opposition than he actually expressed. The reader must decide whether such a singular act of rebellion as a vote against them in 1935, with so much to lose, would have advanced his agenda or hampered it.

Churchill was in a box, not wishing to become an enemy of old colleagues, hoping for office, yet in turmoil, as he frankly admitted a year later: "I confess that I have been occupied with this idea of the great wheels revolving and the great hammers descending day and night in

Germany, making the whole industry of that country an arsenal, welding the whole of its population into one disciplined war machine....I would endure with patience the roar of exultation that would go up when I was proved wrong, because it would lift a load off my heart and off the hearts of many Members. What does it matter who gets exposed or discomfited? If the country is safe, who cares for individual politicians, in or out of office?"[43]

Alas the country was not safe. By the time he uttered those words the disciplined war machine had marched unopposed into the Rhineland.

Chapter 3

The Rhineland:
"They had only to act to win," March 1936

"We dedicate ourselves to achieving an understanding between the peoples of Europe and particularly an understanding with our Western peoples and neighbours. After three years, I believe that, with the present day, the struggle for German equal rights can be regarded as closed....we have no territorial claims to make in Europe." —Hitler to the Reichstag, 7 March 1936

German troops crossing Hohenzollern Bridge over the Rhine, 7 March 1936.
(Bundesarchiv, Bild 183-2006-0315-500)

The Rhineland in western Germany is bordered by the River Rhine in the east and France and the Benelux countries in the west. It includes the industrial Ruhr Valley, the famous cities of Aachen, Bonn, Cologne, Düsseldorf, Essen, Koblenz, Mannheim and Wiesbaden, and several bridgeheads into Germany proper.

At the end of World War I the Rhineland was occupied by the victorious Allies. Though the occupation was set to last through 1935, forces withdrew in 1930 as a good-will gesture to the Weimar Republic.[44] The Allies were authorized to reoccupy the Rhineland any time they considered that Germany had violated the Treaty of Versailles.

In March 1936, a few thousand German troops marched into the Rhineland while a rejoicing German populace waved swastika flags. The soldiers had orders to "turn back and not to resist" if challenged by the all-dominant French Army. Hitler later said that the forty-eight hours following his action were the most tense of his life.[45]

Since the occupied Saarland had been returned to Germany after a plebiscite in January 1935, the Rhineland was Hitler's first foray into territory where he was not permitted. Churchill's defenders correctly cite the Rhineland as confirming his warnings about Hitler. But what Churchill actually proposed to do about it is not as clear.[46]

Two months earlier Churchill had predicted that a Rhineland incursion would raise "a very grave European issue, and no one can tell what would come of it....The League of Nations Union folk, who have done their best to get us disarmed, may find themselves confronted by terrible circumstances."[47]

Hitler's future foreign minister, Joachim von Ribbentrop,[48] recorded how Hitler conceived of slipping the occupation past the Western allies. Summoning Ribbentrop in January, Hitler said: "...it occurred to me last night how we can occupy the Rhineland without any friction. We return to the League!"[49] Germany had left the League of Nations in 1933.

Ribbentrop said he too (of course) had just had this very idea, and suggested that the Germans strike while the French and British were on their weekend holiday. Hitler did so on Saturday March 7th, declaring that France had abrogated the Rhine agreements by a military alliance with Russia "exclusively directed against Germany….the Locarno Rhine Pact has lost its meaning and ceased in practice to exist."[50]

True to plan, Hitler added a sweetener, proposing "a real pacification of Europe between states that are equal in rights" and Germany's return to the League, provided she got back the colonies she had been deprived of at Versailles.

The French Dilemma

The question turned on France. Would she march? Or just dither and do nothing? Anthony Eden,[51] who had replaced Samuel Hoare as foreign secretary in December 1935, was sanguine, declaring that Britain would stand by France and demanding military staff conversations.

Unfortunately for staff conversations, the French military was led by General Gamelin,[52] a "nondescript *fonctionnaire*," as he was described: "…under pressure he became everything a commander ought not to be: indecisive, given to issuing impulsive orders which he almost always countermanded, and timid to and beyond a fault."[53] The French government may have yearned for a way to stop Hitler, but Gamelin and his military colleagues were more worried about stopping him from invading France proper.[54]

The Baldwin government in London believed France was unwilling to act, with or without Britain. Churchill denied this, describing the resolve of French Foreign Minister Pierre Flandin,[55] who met with Churchill in London four days after Hitler's action:

He told me he proposed to demand from the British Government simultaneous mobilisation of the land, sea, and air forces of both countries, and that he had received assurances of support from all the nations of the "Little Entente" [Czechoslovakia, Rumania and Yugoslavia] and from other States. He read out an impressive list of the replies received. There was no doubt that superior strength still lay with the Allies of the former war. They had only to act to win.[56]

Churchill urged Flandin to press Prime Minister Baldwin, who proved unsupportive. He knew little of foreign affairs, he said, but he did know that the British people wanted peace. Flandin replied, if Germany could tear up Locarno, what use were any treaties? The French were resolved, he said, because "everything was at stake." All Flandin asked of his British ally was a "free hand."[57]

Baldwin, who privately doubted that Flandin had the support of his cabinet in Paris, remained adamant even after Flandin modified his entreaty, suggesting merely that Germany be "invited" to leave, pending negotiations which would probably restore the Rhineland to it. Even this was too much for Baldwin: "I have not the right to involve England," he said. Then he hesitated: "Britain is not in a state to go to war." Flandin was deflated, and ministerial meetings in Paris underlined the division among French leaders.[58]

Some have suggested that Flandin never really wanted French military action—merely sanctions by the League of Nations Council. But even sanctions were not forthcoming. Perhaps Flandin merely proposed to convene the League Council, and adopt "sanctions by stages."[59] In any case, Baldwin was unmoved.

The pressure in Britain to avoid action was strong. At a dinner of ex-servicemen in Leicester, one of Churchill's allies, Leo Amery, gave a fiery speech declaring that Britain's very existence was threatened. To the amazement of an observer, the ex-servicemen sided with the Germans, saying in effect, "Why shouldn't they have their own territory back; if they get it, it's no concern of ours."[60]

Publicly, Churchill was being cautious. "I was careful not to derogate in the slightest degree from my attitude of severe though friendly criticism of Government policy," he wrote. The friendliness is more evident than the severity. Neville Chamberlain recorded that Churchill had "suppressed the attack he had intended and made a constructive and helpful speech."[61]

Churchill did urge a "coordinated plan" under the League of Nations to help France challenge the German action. This was denied. Sir Samuel Hoare replied that the necessary participants in such a plan were "totally unprepared from a military point of view." This, one observer noted, "definitely sobered them down."[62]

"No Fresh Perplexities"

Five days after Hitler's action, Baldwin announced, not a new Ministry of Defence or Supply, which Churchill had been urging, but a "Minister for the Coordination of

Defence," which was something less entirely. The job went to Attorney General Sir Thomas Inskip, who knew nothing of the subject, but at least, Chamberlain noted, "would involve us in no fresh perplexities." A British general added: "Thank God we are preserved from Winston Churchill."[63]

Inskip's appointment disappointed Churchill, who, hoping to be called to office, had carefully avoided public criticism of the government. Baldwin, Churchill reminisced, "thought, no doubt, that he had dealt me a politically fatal stroke, and I felt he might well be right."[64]

Having decided that if he could not have office, he would at least have audience, Churchill the next day began a series of fortnightly articles on foreign affairs for the *Evening Standard*. In the first, "Britain, Germany and Locarno," he renewed his call for League of Nations intercession on the Rhineland. Carefully he explained that there was a peaceful way to resolve the problem:

The Germans claim that the Treaty of Locarno has been ruptured by the Franco-Soviet pact. That is their case and it is one that should be argued before the World Court at The Hague. The French have expressed themselves willing to submit this point to arbitration and to abide by the result. Germany should be asked to act in the same spirit and to agree. If the German case is good and the World Court pronounces that the Treaty of Locarno has been vitiated by the Franco-Soviet pact, then clearly the German action, although utterly wrong in method, can not be seriously challenged by the League of Nations.[65]

This is not the defiant voice for which Churchill has been lauded so often. He was not urging military action, but adjudication. But he did warn that if the League failed in its duty, it might cause events to "slide remorselessly downhill towards the pit in which Western civilization might be fatally engulfed."

Churchill continued to urge talks, while also stating—as he always did when it came to negotiating with adversaries—that the Germans must be confronted with supreme strength and resolution:

I desire to see the collective forces of the world invested with overwhelming power. If you are going to depend on a slight margin, one way or the other, you will have war. But if you get five or ten to one on one side, all bound rigorously by the Covenant [of the League] and the conventions which they own, then you may have an opportunity of a settlement which will heal the wounds of the world. Let us have this blessed union of power and of justice: "Agree with thine adversary quickly, whiles thou art in the way with him."[66]

Churchill's next article, "Stop it Now!", did not refer to stopping Hitler but to stopping dithering and hesitation. This was no task for France and Britain alone, he declared. It was a task for all: "There may still be time. Let the States and people who lie in fear of Germany carry their alarms to the League of Nations at Geneva."[67] In the absence of French military action he was falling back on collective security.

Aside from British political considerations, Churchill was attempting to see things from the French viewpoint. The French were "afraid of the Germans," he wrote to *The Times*; France had joined the sanctions against Italy over Italy's 1935 invasion of Abyssinia, and the resulting estrangement had given Hitler this Rhineland opportunity.

In fact Mr. Baldwin's Government, from the very highest motives, endorsed by the country at the General Election, has, without helping Abyssinia at all, got France into grievous trouble which has to be compensated by the precise engagement of our armed forces. Surely in the light of these facts, undisputed as I deem them to be, we might at least judge the French, with whom our fortunes appear to be so decisively linked, with a reasonable understanding....[68]

Did Churchill Waffle?

Churchill favoured a collective response to the Rhineland, and recognized its portents. One event followed the other, as the hard-line Member of Parliament Robert Boothby later recorded: "The military occupation of the Rhineland separated France from her allies in Eastern Europe. The occupation of Austria isolated Czechoslovakia. The betrayal of Czechoslovakia by the West isolated Poland. The defeat of Poland isolated France. The defeat of France isolated Britain. If Britain had been defeated the United States would have been given true and total isolation for the first time."[69]

Churchill certainly would have backed French reoccupation of the Rhineland, at least of the bridgeheads in places like Cologne.[70] When France, rebuffed by Baldwin, proved unwilling to act, he fell back on the League of Nations. Churchill never urged unilateral British action, but he did believe that firmness would cause Hitler to recoil.

There is evidence that Churchill knew all along that the League was toothless, and it has been suggested that he used the League as a way to cloak his balance-of-power politics in the context of the international body.[71] But Churchill's tune did not suddenly change in 1936, it merely evolved. As early as 1933 he had declared:

I believe that we shall find our greatest safety in co-operating with the other Powers of Europe, not taking a leading part, but coming in with all the neutral States....We shall make a great mistake to separate ourselves entirely from them at this juncture. Whatever way we turn there is risk. But the least risk and the greatest help will be found in re-creating the Concert of Europe....[72]

That was not to be. The failure of a concerted response from the Western Allies over the Rhineland was to be repeated as time went on, with western statesmen always hoping each inroad by Hitler would be the last.[73] It is the belief of many thoughtful historians that Churchill said and did nothing about the Rhineland, even in the weeks after he had been denied office.[74] His actions are more complex than that. He did give mixed signals, but did urge solutions. Once France had refused to act, he favoured collective action. His actions were hardly a clarion call.[75] But we must bear in mind also that he was not in office.

Churchill's words on Hitler (Chapter II) did not amount to admiration, except in the narrow sense of Hitler's political skills. There is no doubt that Churchill spoke well of Mussolini, up to 1940.[76] But was this because he admired Fascism, or because he hoped to influence the Italian dictator?

The Rhineland led to Churchill's abandonment of hope in the League of Nations, and increased his efforts to secure collective security through "a coalition of the willing" (to use a more recent and perhaps uncomfortable phrase). The problem was that the willing were few—and demonstrably unwilling to cooperate.

Chapter 4

Corporal Hitler's Dream:
The Austrian *Anschluss*, March 1938

"Don't believe that anyone in the world will hinder me in my decisions! Italy? I am quite clear with Mussolini; with Italy I am on the closest possible terms. England? England will not lift a finger for Austria. And France? Well, two years ago when we marched into the Rhineland with a handful of battalions—at that moment I risked a great deal. If France had marched then we should have been forced to withdraw....But for France it is now too late!"
　　　　　　—Hitler to Schuschnigg, Berchtesgaden, 12 February 1938

Ovation for Hitler in the Reichstag after announcing the Anschluss.
(U.S. Holocaust Memorial Museum, National Archives)

Churchill never denied Germany's grievances over certain clauses of the Versailles Treaty, but he was not conscious of how the Austrians felt. There is little doubt that most Austrians wanted *Anschluss*, a union with Germany, from the time of Versailles on.[77] Churchill did not accept this; he was quite likely wrong.

Austria-Hungary had been dismembered at Versailles; even the Austrian Tyrol and Trieste had gone to Italy in the interest of Italian security. Breaking up the Hapsburg Empire was a priority; to have merged Austria with Germany would have left a larger, more populous Reich than in the Kaiser's time.[78]

Toward *Anschluss*

On 23 March 1931, without informing the League of Nations, Austria and Weimar Germany concluded a customs union, causing protests—but no action—by France and Britain. Churchill grasped the implications:

Beneath the Customs Union lurks the "Anschluss"....France with her dwindling but well-armed population sees the solid German block of 70 millions producing far more than twice her number of military males each year. [If Germany were to annex Austria] Czechoslovakia will not only have the indigestible morsel in its interior, but will be surrounded on three sides by other Germans.[79]

Of course, Churchill added, if the customs union were purely economic and not political, it might deprive "the much more dangerous Hitler movement of its mainspring." On this thin strand the isolationist Hearst press in America headlined his article, "Austro-German Union Would Aid World Peace Says Winston Churchill."[80]

Churchill consistently maintained that Hitler would recoil if confronted with force. When Austrian Nazis attempted a coup in July 1934, Austria defeated it, arresting the plotters. The Anglo-French took no particular notice, but Hitler temporarily halted his propaganda campaign for union, and Austrian Nazis ceased for a time their campaign of murders and bombings.[81]

In May 1935 Hitler declared that he had no evil intent toward anyone. The Reich had guaranteed French borders, he said, including Alsace-Lorraine. Germany "neither intends nor wishes to interfere in the internal affairs of Austria, to annex Austria, or to conclude an *Anschluss*."

The Times editor Geoffrey Dawson called Hitler's speech "reasonable, straightforward, and comprehensive.... [it] may fairly constitute the basis of a complete settlement with Germany." But Nazi street gangs were again at large in Vienna.[82]

A few hours after his speech Hitler took less public actions: the Ministry of Defence became the Ministry of War under commander-in-chief von Blomberg; Goering was sent to head the Luftwaffe, Raeder the Navy. "The tempo of the Reich's martial music was accelerando." wrote William Manchester. "Had *The Times* known of this, Dawson's enthusiasm might have been tempered, but there can be little doubt that the paper's course would have remained unaltered."[83] Ten months later Hitler digested the Rhineland.

Hitler Approaches Churchill

In early 1937, with Hitler's approval, Ribbentrop invited Churchill to the German Embassy to explain why the Reich was no threat to Britain. It is a mystery why Hitler approved a meeting with the Englishman he had refused to see in 1932, one who was still politically powerless.

Leading Churchill to a large wall map, Ribbentrop showed Hitler's desiderata: Poland, Ukraine and Byelorussia, a "Greater German Reich" of 760,000 square miles (Germany was then 182,000, Britain 89,000). The return of former German colonies was desirable, but "not cardinal." In exchange for British acquiescence, "Germany would stand guard for the British Empire in all its greatness and extent."

It was true, Churchill replied, that…

…we were on bad terms with Soviet Russia and that we hated Communism as much as Hitler did, but…even if France were safeguarded Great Britain would never disinterest herself in the fortunes of the Continent to an extent which would enable Germany to gain the domination of Central and Eastern Europe. We were actually standing before the map when I said this. Ribbentrop turned abruptly away. He then said, "In that case, war is inevitable. There is no way out. The Führer is resolved. Nothing will stop him and nothing will stop us…."

I thought it right to say to the German Ambassador—in fact, I remember the words well, "When you talk of war, which no doubt would be general war, you must not underrate England. She is a curious country, and few foreigners can understand her mind. Do not judge by the attitude of the present Administration. Once a great cause is presented to the people all kinds of unexpected actions might be taken by this very Government and by the British nation." And I repeated, "Do not underrate England. She is very clever. If you plunge us all into

another Great War she will bring the whole world against
you, like last time." At this the Ambassador rose in heat
and said, "Ah, England may be very clever, but this time
she will not bring the world against Germany."[84]

Hitler Strikes

The failed Nazi coup in 1934 had not changed
Hitler's objectives, but easing Austria into the Reich would
take a bit longer. The final preparations, "Case Otto", were
completed in February 1938, when Hitler personally
replaced von Blomberg as head of the army and installed
loyal men in key posts: General Keitel as Army chief of
staff, Ribbentrop as foreign minister. On February 12th,
Austrian Chancellor Kurt von Schuschnigg[85] was
summoned to Berchtesgaden, where Hitler confronted him
with threats of immediate invasion.

Schuschnigg was wily, and by no means a liberal
democrat. As head of the right-wing Fatherland Front he
ruled by decree, an authoritarian with anti-Semitic leanings
similar to Hitler's. But he was determined to preserve
Austrian independence. Defying Hitler's threats, he
scheduled a plebiscite to settle the question on March 13th,
hoping to get a "no" vote by legalizing the outlawed
Socialists and raising the voting age to 24 in the belief that
Austrian youth was pro-Nazi.

He was not given the chance. Austrian Nazis seized
control of the government on March 11th, cancelling the
referendum; Nazi troops entered the country, and Hitler
formally annexed Austria on March 12th. In a plebiscite a
few weeks later, 99.8% supposedly voted "Ja."

Churchill argued that two-thirds of Austrians were
opposed to the union, but his only evidence was the reports

of upper-class anti-Nazis.[86] His cousin Unity Mitford told him he was badly misinformed, that the only Austrians against union were the aristocrats: "*Anschluss* with the Reich was the great wish of the entire German population of the Austro-Hungarian Empire, long before the war and long before Hitler was even born, though the English press would make one believe that it was the Führer who invented the idea."[87]

Unity Mitford was a Hitler sycophant, but in this case she was probably right. Yet from the standpoint of *realpolitik,* it mattered not what the Austrians wanted: the *Anschluss* violated the Versailles Treaty. It could have been resisted, and resistance might have precluded much that followed.

Churchill's Prescriptions

Although the Treaties of Versailles and St. Germain specifically forbade the union, Anglo-French reaction was muted. No military confrontation took place, and even Mussolini, whom Hitler had worried might object, made no protest. Two days after the annexation, Churchill addressed the House of Commons. His analysis of Hitler's accomplishment proved exacting:

Vienna is the centre of all the communications of all the countries which formed the old Austro-Hungarian Empire, and of all the countries lying to the south-east of Europe. A long stretch of the Danube is now in German hands. This mastery of Vienna gives to Nazi Germany military and economic control of the whole of the communications of south-eastern Europe, by road, by river, and by rail....the three countries of the Little Entente may be called Powers of the second rank, but they are very vigorous States, and united they are a Great Power....Rumania has the oil; Yugoslavia has the minerals and raw materials. Both have large armies; both are mainly supplied with munitions from Czechoslovakia.[88]

Only months later Mr. Chamberlain would refer to Czechoslovakia as "a far-away country...of whom we know nothing." Churchill might have been anticipating the Prime Minister when he added, with heavy irony:

To English ears, the name of Czechoslovakia sounds outlandish. No doubt they are only a small democratic State, no doubt they have an army only two or three times as large as ours, no doubt they have a munitions supply only three times as great as that of Italy, but still they are a virile people; they have their treaty rights, they have a line of fortresses, and they have a strongly manifested will to live freely. Czechoslovakia is at this moment isolated, both in the economic and in the military sense.[89]

Churchill did not propose military action, but there is no doubt that he wanted to confront Hitler with a union of powers: "What is there ridiculous about collective security? The only thing that is ridiculous about it is that we have not got it." He then proposed how to get it:

If a number of States were assembled around Great Britain and France in a solemn treaty for mutual defence against aggression; if they had their forces marshalled in what you may call a Grand Alliance....if that were sustained, as it would be, by the moral sense of the world; and if it were done in the year 1938 and, believe me, it may be the last

*chance there will be for doing it, then I say that you might
even now arrest this approaching war....let those who wish
to reject it ponder well and earnestly upon what will
happen to us if, when all else has been thrown to the
wolves, we are left to face our fate alone.*[90]

Churchill returned to this theme a few days later.
Now, he said, was the time of reckoning. The western
allies...

*...will carry their action as far as may be necessary to
deter or, failing that, to resist, further instances of
unprovoked aggression.....The urgency of the undertaking
arises from the fact that the hope of producing peace by
concerted action is greater in 1938 than it would be in
1939, and far greater than in 1940. To continue
delaying...would seem to make war certain at a later
date.*[91]

"Those who wished to reject" Churchill's calls were
running the government. Thus the question of whether the
Western Allies could have bucked up Schuschnigg by
backing Austrian resistance and mobilizing was left
unanswered. To Mr. Chamberlain, the very idea was
ridiculous—and so was a defence of Czechoslovakia:

*"...the plan of the 'Grand Alliance,' as Winston calls it,
had occurred to me long before he mentioned it....It is a
very attractive idea; indeed, there is almost everything to
be said for it until you come to examine its practicability.
From that moment its attraction vanishes. You have only to
look at the map, to see that nothing that France or we
could do could possibly save Czechoslovakia from being*

overrun by the Germans, if they wanted to do it. The
Austrian frontier is practically open; the great Skoda
munition works are within easy bombing distance of the
German aerodromes, the railways all pass through
German territory, Russia is 100 miles away. Therefore we
could not help Czechoslovakia—she would simply be a
pretext for going to war with Germany. That we could not
think of unless we had a reasonable prospect of being able
to beat her to her knees in a reasonable time, and of that I
see no sign. I have therefore abandoned any idea of giving
guarantees to Czechoslovakia, or the French in connection
with her obligations to that country."[92]

A cynic would note that Chamberlain would soon
give a guarantee to Poland, farther away and far less
defensible. Basing so momentous decision on geography
alone is incomprehensible. "In modern wars of great
nations or alliances particular areas are not defended only
by local exertions," Churchill commented. "The whole
vast balance of the war-front is involved. This is still more
true of policy before war begins and while it may still be
averted."[93]

The prospect of a mobilized Royal Navy and French
Army, together with either Austria's eighteen divisions or
the formidable Czech army dug in on their borders, might
have given pause even to Hitler—who was only acting, as
he admitted to Schuschnigg on 12 February, because he
was certain that Britain and France would "not lift a
finger."

Churchill added: "How erroneous Mr.
Chamberlain's private and earnest reasoning appears when
we cast our minds forward to the guarantee he was to give
to Poland within a year, after all the strategic value of

Czechoslovakia had been cast away, and Hitler's power and prestige had almost doubled!"[94]

German Vulnerability

There was another reason favouring resistance: the Wehrmacht, marching into Austria, was experiencing a mechanical breakdown rate of up to 30%.[95] And this was not its only problem:

Officers and men arrived late to their posts and were misassigned or simply untrained for their duties. Wagons and motorized vehicles were frequently missing, inadequate for their tasks or unusable. Indeed, the German VII Army Corps alone described its supplementary motorized vehicle situation as "nahezu katastrophal" (almost catastrophic), with approximately 2800 motorized vehicles which were either missing or unusable. Nor was the situation any better regarding horses, the prime mover of the Wehrmacht. Once inside Austria, the difficulties were aggravated through a completely inadequate road and rail network and the huge numbers of men and materiel attempting to push through. Poor discipline, lack of training, and outright incompetence worsened matters, as did mechanical breakdowns and lack of fuel. The result was that divisions, regiments, and battalions were completely torn asunder; they ceased to be combat units.

Like some great malfunctioning clockwork, the Wehrmacht lurched and shuddered towards the Austrian capital. Only a few parts of it finally grated to a halt in the suburbs of Vienna one week later. Even this dismal performance was only possible due to vital and essential assistance rendered to the Wehrmacht by Austrian gas stations, and shipping and rail services. Without this help, Hitler's victory parade on the Ringstraße would have been conspicuously devoid of German troops and armour. Nevertheless, as with the North Vietnamese Tet Offensive thirty years later, operational disaster does not equal military disaster. The Nazi propaganda machine, parts of which were busy running down German soldiers in their rush to get to Vienna on 12 and 13 March, would prove as successful as it had ever been.[96]

"A triumphal entry into Vienna had been the Austrian Corporal's dream," Churchill later wrote. "Hitler himself, motoring through Linz, saw the traffic jam, and was infuriated....He rated his generals, and they answered back. They reminded him of his refusal to listen to Fritsch and his warnings that Germany was not in a position to undertake the risk of a major conflict."[97]

It is unfortunate that notice of these deficiencies eluded, or—since their observers were reporting from Vienna, were ignored—by the British and French governments, and papered over by Nazi propaganda. Even Churchill did not comment *at the time* on this extraordinary display of military incompetence. It might have made a difference a few months later.

The day before the *Anschluss*, Hermann Goering received the Czech Ambassador in Berlin: "I give you my word of honour," he said affably, "that Czechoslovakia has nothing to fear from the Reich."[98]

Chapter 5

Last Chance at Munich:
The Case for Resistance, 1938

"I have watched this famous island descending incontinently, fecklessly, the stairway which leads to a dark gulf. It is a fine broad stairway at the beginning, but after a bit the carpet ends. A little farther on there are only flagstones, and a little farther on still these break beneath your feet. Look back over the last five years....if mortal catastrophe should overtake the British Nation and the British Empire, historians a thousand years hence will still be baffled by the mystery of our affairs. They will never understand how it was that a victorious nation, with everything in hand, suffered themselves to be brought low, and to cast away all that they had gained by measureless sacrifice and absolute victory—gone with the wind!" —Churchill, House of Commons, 24 March 1938

Heston aerodrome, 30 September 1938: Neville Chamberlain waves the paper signed by Hitler and him at Munich, vowing that Germany and Britain were resolved never to go to war again. (Wikimedia)

In September 1938 Hitler declared that the continued presence of the ethnic German Sudetenland within Czechoslovakia was intolerable, and threatened to go to war were it not incorporated in the Reich. At first agreeing to a plebiscite, he then rejected it, and on 30 September, Britain and France, after much soul-searching but without consulting the Czechs, signed an agreement giving Hitler what he wanted. The Sudetenland was annexed by the Reich, and six months later Hitler absorbed, or turned into puppet states, the remainder of Czechoslovakia.

I do not here record the detailed history of the Munich Pact, so exhaustively recounted already. Nor is this an attempt to pillory Neville Chamberlain, an easy target for generations of second-guessers. He acted in the hope of preserving peace; he was wrong in key respects. He did spur rearmament in the year before the war, and he did support Churchill from the hard days of May 1940 until his own death six months later. Churchill was grateful for this.

My purpose is rather to weigh Churchill's critique at the time, which stands on two legs. 1) Hitler in 1938 was by no means all-powerful: Czech defences were formidable; on Germany's flanks the French army was mobilising; the Royal Navy was mobilized. 2) Hitler in 1938 was not ready for a protracted war, and politically vulnerable.

Churchill took up his argument only two weeks after the *Anschluss*, knowing that the threat was now to Czechoslovakia. In the event of "an act of violent aggression" on the Czechs, he said, "then we should feel, on this occasion, and in this emergency, bound to act with France in resisting it." He did not believe that there was an immediate danger of a major land war. He offered two reasons: first, "Germany is not ready this year for such an ordeal as a major land war"; second, "I cannot see that it would be in the interest of the rulers of Germany to provoke such a war." He added that if the allies did not resist now, "we shall only prepare the day when we shall have to stand up to them under far more adverse conditions....Where shall we be a year hence? Where shall we be in 1940?"[99]

Churchill's military rationale was sound. There is no indication in the Churchill record that he knew of any plots against Hitler; but his surmise that a major war would not be in Hitler's interest was correct.

Yet still today we are regularly told that the Munich agreement was necessary and wise because it gave Britain more time to arm. We are less rarely reminded that Munich also gave Germany more time to arm, to neutralize a potential enemy through a treaty with the Soviet Union, and to reap a military bonanza in Czechoslovakia. If fighting Hitler in 1938 was so ludicrous a concept, what was there about fighting him in 1939-40 that made it preferable? Was it the eradication of Poland in three weeks, the Low Countries in sixteen days, France in six weeks?

Chamberlain's defenders argue that Britain and France could not have sent armies into landlocked Czechoslovakia. Even Churchill admitted this: "It surely did not take much thought...that the British Navy and the French Army could not be deployed on the Bohemian mountain front."[100] But there was more to the equation than that. There was the Royal Navy and the French Army, on Germany's borders. Czechoslovakia proper had formidable defences—see "The Balance of Forces" below.

On 18 June 1938 Hitler informed his generals that Czechoslovakia would be attacked to expand "Lebensraum" for Greater Germany, and Germanic peoples trapped in the Czech Sudetenland. Czech Nazis duly began a campaign of civil unrest, accompanied by shrill denunciations from Berlin. In September Hitler labelled Czechoslovakia a "fraudulent state," and Mussolini declared that he supported Hitler.

Hitler was flabbergasted, however, when Prime Minister Neville Chamberlain offered to fly to meet him and settle all differences at Berchtesgaden on September 15th. From there, with Hitler's apparent agreement, Chamberlain offered Czech President Edouard Beneš a security guarantee provided Beneš accepted the awarding, by plebiscite, of the Sudetenland to the Reich.

Meeting Hitler again at Bad Godesberg on the 23rd, Chamberlain was astonished to learn that Hitler had reneged. The Führer now demanded that the Czechs accept German occupation of the Sudetenland in five days, later setting this back to October 1st "out of respect" for Chamberlain. On hearing this, Czechoslovakia mobilized for war.

The Balance of Forces

Months before, Hitler was at pains to assure his anxious military, only too aware of the Reich's military situation: "I will take action," he told Keitel, his Army chief of staff,[101] "only if I am firmly convinced, as in the case of the demilitarised zone [Rhineland] and the entry into Austria that France will not march, and that therefore England will not intervene."[102]

At his Nuremberg trial, Keitel was asked by the Czech representative: "Would the Reich have attacked Czechoslovakia in 1938 if the Western Powers had stood by Prague?" "Certainly not," the Field Marshal replied.

"We were not strong enough militarily. The object of Munich was to get Russia out of Europe, to gain time, and to complete the German armaments."[103]

Serious studies of the balance of forces in the 1930s supports Keitel's reply. In fact, the German army in mid-1938 was just beginning its rearmament program:

It possessed only three armored divisions, all of which were equipped with light tanks, obsolete even by standards of the time. One year later, it would possess six panzer divisions, which it would buttress with the first runs of Mark III and IV medium tanks. The Germans would find the Czech tanks they seized in March 1939 quite useful, [providing] three of the ten panzer divisions that invaded France in May 1940....It is hard to see how 1938's three divisions of light tanks could have achieved the smashing victories Hitler promised in either autumn 1938 or spring 1939.[104]

The Reich's air force and navy were no more ready than the army. The Luftwaffe was only beginning to develop the fast new aircraft that would dominate France in 1940. In 1938, its operationally-ready rate just topped 50 percent, while most of its pilots remained untrained."[105] The navy possessed only three pocket battleships and just a handful of U-boats, later to be so feared. "The German navy could not even execute an invasion of Norway, which succeeded only by the barest margins in April 1940, at a cost of virtually the entire German fleet."[106.]

The economic situation was equally doubtful, strained in part by construction of the "Westwall" (Siegfried Line) opposite the Maginot Line on the French border. Germany's only abundant raw material was coal and some iron ore, but French and Swedish ore was essential. Oil, rubber, manganese and aluminium were in short supply or non-existent.[107] A British naval blockade would have severely curtailed imports of such resources. As the Reich Defence Committee reported at the height of the Munich crisis:

...in consequence of Wehrmacht demands and unlimited construction on the Westwall, so tense a situation in the economic sector occurred (coal, supplies for industries, harvest of potatoes and turnips, food supplies) that the continuation of the tension past October 10 would have made a catastrophe inevitable.[108]

What about the opposition? Williamson Murray writes: "While in a strategic sense the Czech position seemed hopeless, tactically their country was far more defensible than Poland would prove the following year....Moreover, Czech equipment was much more up-to-date than that of the Poles."[109] All this was known to Churchill at the time: "The Czechs had a million and a half men armed behind the strongest fortress line in Europe, and equipped by a highly organised and powerful industrial machine. The French Army was partly mobilized, and, albeit reluctantly, the French Ministers were prepared to honour their obligations to Czechoslovakia."[110]

Hitler Hesitates

On September 26th, with the Czechs mobilized and war likely, a delegation of high-ranking military leaders asked to meet with the Führer. Denied an audience, they drafted a memorandum, published in November. Churchill described it in his memoirs:

Chapter I stresses the divergences between the political and military leadership of the Third Reich, and declares that the low morale of the German population renders it incapable of sustaining a European war....Chapter II describes the bad condition of the Reichswehr and... "the absence of discipline." Chapter III enumerates the various deficiencies in German armaments, dwelling upon the defects in the Siegfried Line, so hurriedly constructed, and the lack of fortifications in the Aix-la-Chapelle and Saarbruck areas. Fear is expressed of an incursion into Belgium by the French troops concentrated around Givet. Finally, emphasis is laid on the shortage of officers....in the event of a general mobilisation no fewer than eighteen divisions would find themselves devoid of trained subordinate commanders....

A military appreciation about Czechoslovakia in the Appendix states that the Czechoslovak Army, even if fighting without allies, could hold out for three months, and that Germany would need to retain covering forces on the Polish and French frontiers as well as on the Baltic and North Sea coasts, and to keep a force of at least a quarter of a million troops in Austria to guard against popular risings and a possible Czechoslovak offensive. Finally, the General Staff believed that it was highly improbable that hostilities would remain localised during the three-month period.[111]

British attitudes were likewise hardening. On the 26th, at the behest of his Cabinet, Chamberlain informed

Hitler that if the Czechs rejected terms and France was involved Britain would stand by France. At midnight on September 27th the Admiralty ordered mobilisation of the Fleet. Hearing of this, a thoughtful Hitler said to Goering: "the English fleet might shoot after all,"[112] and postponed German mobilisation.

If the Royal Navy gave Hitler pause, so too did his own people. At dusk on September 27th, a motorised division rolled through Berlin, where the Führer on a balcony appeared to take their salute, the hour chosen to catch crowds of Berliners headed home at the end of the day's work. But according to an American reporter, William Shirer, "they ducked into the subways, refused to look on, and the handful that did stood at the curb in utter silence....there weren't two hundred people....Hitler looked grim, then angry, and soon went inside....What I've seen tonight almost rekindles a little faith in the German people. They are dead set against war."[113]

Unfortunately, Neville Chamberlain wasn't there to see. And, unbeknown to his Cabinet, the Prime Minister had just written Hitler, lauding their close relationship and mutual respect, and proposing a conference between Britain, Germany, Czechoslovakia, France and Italy.

Chamberlain was actually speaking in the House of Commons when an aide showed him Hitler's invitation to meet the next day in Munich. Triumphantly, he vowed to be there. The House broke into cheers. Magnanimous to the last, Churchill rose, shook Chamberlain's hand, and wished him "God-speed." Later a colleague said that since Churchill had been involved in no intrigues, he was perfectly entitled to support Chamberlain if a firm line were taken. Churchill growled: "The last word has not been spoken yet."[114]

The Plot Against Hitler

Chamberlain's agreement to meet Hitler at Munich saved more than he realized. There was every reason to believe that, had Britain and France taken a strong line and vowed to resist the occupation of the Sudetenland, Hitler would have been eliminated by German leaders.

The plot rose to a high level, involving Admiral Wilhelm Canaris, chief of the Abwehr (military intelligence); his second-in-command, Lt. Col. Hans Oster; General Erwin von Witzleben, chief of the Third Army Corps; Chief of the General Staff Franz Halder and former chief Ludwig Beck; Wehrmacht commander General Walter von Brauchitsch, State Secretary Ernst von Weizsacker of the Foreign Ministry; and Hjalmar Schacht, President of the Reichsbank, who had agreed to head a provisional government.[115]

Their instrument was a crack team of hand-picked anti-Nazis, half of them serving officers, commanded by Capt. Friedrich Heinz of the Abwehr. Witzleben wanted them to arrest Hitler and hold him for trial for "taking Germany into an unwanted war that senior military leaders, including Luftwaffe chief Harman Goering, opposed." Heinz and Oster, convinced that the Führer alive was a war in prospect, secretly planned to open fire, killing Hitler on the spot.[116]

The raid was to take place after the expiration of Hitler's original deadline to invade Czechoslovakia, September 28th. Simultaneously, Berlin police would arrest other top Nazis; General Walter von Brockdorf, commander of the 23rd Infantry Division in Potsdam, had promised to neutralize the Berlin SS.[117]

One person tried to make Chamberlain was aware of the plot. Ewald von Kleist, an ardent anti-Nazi, was sent to London in August to leak the news in a hope of stiffening British resolve. The Prime Minister was unimpressed. Kleist, he told Halifax, "reminds me of the Jacobites at the Court of France in King William's time and I think that we must discount a good deal of what he says."[118] The Prime Minister must also have discounted his own intelligence reports: Britain had been receiving news of the coup since July.

Given Chamberlain's attitude, the conspiracy had no traction in London, and the planners were continually upset by events. During Chamberlain's September 15th visit to Berchtesgaden, Oster and his colleagues were more concerned that *Hitler* might back down than Chamberlain. They were heartened at Bad Godesberg, when Hitler gave Chamberlain an ultimatum they were sure Britain and France would never accept.[119] They were wrong again.

On September 28th, as the raiding party was drawing arms, Hitler invited Chamberlain to Munich. Two days later, the four powers (absent Czechoslovakia) agreed on immediate occupation of the Sudetenland and a plebiscite (which never occurred) later. On October 3rd the plotters gathered at Witzleben's Berlin mansion and "tossed our lovely plans and projects into the fire. Peace in our time? Let us put it a bit more realistically: Chamberlain saved Hitler."[120] Later, Canaris, von Witzleben, Oster, von Kleist and others were executed for treason.

By the time he wrote his memoirs, Churchill had learned the details. "There can be no doubt," he wrote, "of the existence of the plot at this moment, and of serious measures taken to make it effective. By the beginning of

September [Halder says] we had taken the necessary steps to immunize Germany from this madman. At this time the prospect of war filled the great majority of the German people with horror."[121]

"An Awful Milestone"

Returning triumphantly from Munich, Chamberlain was hailed as a peace-giver who had saved the world. He brought with him a sheet of paper, signed by Hitler and himself, signifying "the desire of our two peoples never to go to war with one another again." Cynics might have noted that the word was "desire," and not "promise." Churchill's description of events in Parliament was not broadly welcomed:

All is over. Silent, mournful, abandoned, broken, Czechoslovakia recedes into the darkness. She has suffered in every respect by her association with the western democracies and with the League of Nations, of which she has always been an obedient servant. We are in the presence of a disaster of the first magnitude.....

I do not grudge our loyal, brave people, who were ready to do their duty no matter what the cost, who never flinched under the strain of last week....but they should know the truth. They should know that there has been gross neglect and deficiency in our defences; they should know that we have sustained a defeat without a war, the consequences of which will travel far with us along our road; they should know that we have passed an awful milestone in our history, when the whole equilibrium of Europe has been deranged, and that the terrible words have for the time being been pronounced against the western democracies: "Thou art weighed in the balance and found wanting."[122]

Hindsight is cheap, and far too easily indulged. Neville Chamberlain was a decent man, trying his best, "according to his lights" as Churchill put it, to avoid an awful struggle, the very idea of which—until perhaps 1938—appalled the British people. Many have argued that, by surrendering in 1938, Chamberlain made it possible to fight in 1939. Subsequent events tend to bring this idea into question.

There is abundant evidence that Churchill was right: that Munich produced a demoralized France, a far more powerful Germany, and a politically unassailable Hitler. Within six months Czechoslovakia, which had been ready to fight if only she was supported, was torn asunder by Germany, Poland and Hungary, and with it her vital arms industry. Ironically, as Williamson Murray noted, the Skoda Works in Czechoslovakia "would remain the last major industrial concern still producing armaments for the Wehrmacht in 1945."[123]

Of course we were not present in 1938. We don't know the mood of the people, the soldiers, the politicians. We never—indeed even Churchill never—met the formidable Führer face to face. We will never know the outcome of the plot, or the precise scenario if the West had stood its ground. But if we seek the truth, we are obliged to consider Churchill's prescriptions—which were, characteristically, far from baseless.

Chapter 6

The Russian Enigma:
"Favourable Reference to the Devil"

"I cannot forecast to you the action of Russia. It is a riddle wrapped in a mystery inside an enigma: but perhaps there is a key. That key is Russian national interest. It cannot be in accordance with the interest or the safety of Russia that Germany should plant itself upon the shores of the Black Sea, or that it should overrun the Balkan States and subjugate the Slavonic peoples of South-Eastern Europe. That would be contrary to the historic life-interests of Russia."
—Churchill, London, 1 October 1939

Hitler: *"The scum of the earth, I believe?"* Stalin: *"The bloody assassin of the workers, I presume?"* Cartoonist David Low following the attack on Poland, Evening Standard, *London, 20 September 1939.*

As Churchill had predicted, Munich sealed Czechoslovakia's fate. On 14 March 1939, Catholic fascists proclaimed an independent, pro-Nazi republic of Slovakia. The next day Ruthenia seceded, only to be occupied by Hitler's ally Hungary. Summoned to Berlin, Czech President Emil Hácha, threatened with the bombing of Prague, experienced a heart attack. Revived by Hitler's doctor, he agreed to German occupation of the rest of his country, which was renamed the Protectorate of Bohemia and Moravia—an arrangement which "in its unctuous mendacity was remarkable even for the Nazis."[124] In an ironic sequel, Poland occupied Zaolzie, a small enclave with an ethnic Polish minority. Left out since Munich, the Russians were only spectators; they would not be denied when Poland fell a few months later.

Ups and Downs with Ivan

From the time Hitler marched on the Rhineland, Churchill had pondered Anglo-Russian cooperation. The historian Donald Cameron Watt wrote: "He fell into the clutches of Ivan Maisky,[125] the Soviet ambassador in London…writing to Viscount Cecil of the need to 'organise a European mass and, perhaps, a world mass which will confront…the heavily armed unmoral dictatorships.'"[126]

Maisky was clever and worldly, practised in English ways, spoke perfect English, and had cultivated a relationship with Randolph Churchill. Like his superior, Soviet Foreign Minister Maxim Litvinov, he was Jewish, and no admirer of Hitler. In February 1936 he invited Churchill to a film on Red Army manoeuvres. The two held the first of many private chats during the Rhineland crisis. At a reception in November 1937, Churchill broke off a conversation with King George VI to rejoin an animated discussion with Maisky, which the King had broken up, thinking Churchill wished to be rescued.[127]

But "fell into the clutches" is very wide of the mark. Churchill loathed and feared the Soviet Union, and it was a huge decision for him to court Maisky. Yet Churchill could add and subtract, and he needed the help. He acted for big reasons, and he explained them. In the event, his forebodings about the USSR would be proven entirely correct.

On 5 November 1936, Churchill gave a speech criticising Soviet involvement in the Spanish Civil War, but ending by describing "another Russia, which only wishes to be left alone in peace," and play a part in preserving that peace.

Maisky complained of his take on Russia's role in Spain. Churchill politely suggested that Maisky concentrate on "the latter part of my references to your government"—the collective security part.[128] "I fought with all my strength against communism," he said in 1938. But now, "Communism does not pose such a threat to the Empire. On the contrary, now the greatest threat to the British Empire is Nazism, with its doctrine of world domination by Berlin."[129]

After the Wehrmacht occupied Austria, Moscow proposed extending the Franco-Soviet pact to Britain, recreating, as William Manchester wrote, "the entente which had declared war on the Kaiser's Second Reich in 1914 and which would have defeated Germany and Austria, without American help, had the Bolshevik revolution not shattered it three years later."[130] Some saw in this proposal a way to stop Hitler short of all-out war. In Whitehall it met, Churchill recalled, "with little warmth…." [Chamberlain] "was both sceptical and depressed. He profoundly disagreed with my interpretation of the dangers ahead and the means of combating them."[131]

Throughout the summer and early autumn, Chamberlain stalled or spoke in vague generalities to an increasingly frustrated Maisky. No Soviet representative was invited to Munich. Later Chamberlain tried to suggest that the USSR had been consulted. Maisky responded with a pointed memorandum, copied to Churchill, which under the circumstances was justified:

...the "contacts" which the British Government had with the Soviet Government [did not feature] a single case of consultation with the Soviet Government on the steps or measures contemplated by the British or by the British and French Governments in connection with the crisis. Therefore, all attempts which are being made at the present time to create an impression that the Soviet Government had something to do with the Anglo-French Plan of the 13th September or with the Munich "settlement" are absolutely false. [132]

"Decision at Last"

Believing Poland to be next on Hitler's hit list, Britain and France on 31 March 1939 issued a guarantee of Polish independence. "Here was decision at last," Churchill wrote, "taken at the worst possible moment and on the least satisfactory ground...." [133] It would lead eventually to war; it did not at this point express a fully formed resolve.

The pledge was ambiguously worded, symbolising a growing disconnect between the Prime Minister and his government. While his colleagues looked upon it as a warning to Hitler, Chamberlain saw it as a way to renew the Munich negotiations.

The Prime Minister's approach was represented by the establishment press: *The Times* explained that the guarantee committed Britain only to "fair and free negotiation." It did not "defend every inch of the present frontiers of Poland. [Chamberlain's] repeated references to free negotiation imply that he thinks that there are problems in which adjustments are still necessary." It was not a political challenge to the Germans. "It is, on the contrary, an appeal to their better nature."[134]

Churchill was having none of *The Times*'s calm assurances. He doubted the Polish guarantee would stop Hitler, but was still hoping an understanding with Russia would win the day. His colleague Harold Nicolson recalled an episode outside the Commons chamber on April 3rd:

I am seized upon by Winston and taken down to the lower smoking room with Maisky and Lloyd George. Winston adopts the direct method of attack. "Now look here Mr. Ambassador, if we are to make a success of this new policy we require the help of Russia. Now I don't care for your system and I never have, but the Poles and the Romanians like it even less. Although they might be prepared at a pinch to let you in, they would certainly want some assurances that you would eventually get out. Can you give us such assurances?".... Maisky [whose answer Nicolson did not record, takes the line that Russia will not come in to any coalition which includes Italy and that they will have no confidence in France or ourselves if we start flirting with Italy and opening negotiations with Mussolini. Winston takes the line that the main enemy is Germany and that it is always a mistake to allow one's enemies to acquire even unreliable allies.[135]

So much for the notion that Churchill had fallen into Maisky's clutches. His ringing words expressed the difference he drew between Hitler and other tyrants, redolent of his private quip two years later, after the Germans had invaded Russia: "If Hitler invaded Hell I would at least make a favourable reference to the Devil in the House of Commons."[136]

Chamberlain's Soviet Dilemma

Chamberlain's colleague Leo Amery was sure the PM would never deal with Russia: "The trouble with Neville is that he is being pushed into a policy which he does not like and hates abandoning the last bridges which might still enable him to renew his former policy." Chamberlain believed, Amery wrote accurately, that the Poles "had a very considerable distrust of Russia."[137] And this was a good excuse to not to get serious with the Soviets.

Unfortunately, on April 14th the French put the cat among the chickens by telling the Soviets they would agree to a specific military treaty. Four days later Litvinov put the fox among the piglets by proposing a sweeping Anglo-French-Soviet alliance, defending each other and all eastern European nations on the Soviet border from the Baltic to the Black Sea. The Permanent Undersecretary for Foreign Affairs, Alexander Cadogan, a Chamberlain backer who often excoriated Churchill, described the Russian offer as "extremely inconvenient."[138]

Chamberlain's Cabinet was interested. Admiral Lord Chatfield said "it would be disastrous if the Soviet Union made an alliance with Germany." Halifax dismissed that ever happening, but could not get the Soviets to accept a less precise agreement: for Moscow it was mutual assistance or nothing. In the Commons, Lloyd George deplored Chamberlain's desire "to do without Russia." French Prime Minister Daladier wondered why Halifax and Chamberlain were making "so much fuss." A Gallup poll in June would ask, "Do you favour a military alliance between Britain, France and Russia?" Eighty-four percent would respond yes.[139]

In Moscow, discussions dragged on between British Ambassador Sir William Seeds and Litvinov. On the morning of May 3rd the canny Russian asked what the British had meant by promising Poland "all support in their power." Litvinov, wrote R.A.C. Parker, "showed his normal fluency and self-possession. Seeds was surprised when next day's papers announced that he had been replaced as Commissar for Foreign Affairs by V.M. Molotov. This replaced a jovial, communicative advocate of collective security [with] one of the toughest negotiators of the twentieth century." Litvinov's departure also spelled the end of Maisky's influence; from then on, he was kept at arms-length by Moscow, and told nothing.[140]

Russia, Churchill said then, "has pursued a cold policy of self-interest." Later he wrote that the dismissal of Litvinov "registered the abandonment by the Kremlin of all faith in a security pact with the Western Powers and in the possibility of organising an Eastern front against Germany."[141]

"Russian National Interest"

Experience had convinced the Russians that British leaders were really not serious about an alliance. Trying to reassure them, London sent William Strang, head of the

Central Department of the Foreign Office, to Moscow in June. But Halifax, though personally invited by Molotov, never ventured to visit. "The despatch of an official, however distinguished, on such a critical occasion was no substitute for the Foreign Secretary," wrote a Halifax biographer. "Nor did it escape attention that Chamberlain, who had flown three times to see Hitler, betrayed no eagerness to establish contact with Stalin."[142]

Churchill was adamant for a Soviet alliance. Chamberlain was not. Any alliance with the West, Molotov and even Litvinov insisted, must embrace the entire western border of Russia. The clear implication was that the Western powers look the other way if the Soviets in their wisdom felt obliged to rescue the Baltic States or Poland from danger. On May 21st, for example, Molotov asked: "How were eastern European states who did not wish Soviet aid to be protected from German occupation? Finland, Estonia and Latvia would not accept guarantees against Germany. What would happen if states bordering on the Soviet Union collapsed under German attack or, as in the case of Czechoslovakia in March, 'invited' German forces to enter in response to German threats?" The British had no reply.

During the Czech crisis, Litvinov had suggested that Romania might allow passage of Soviet forces if the League of Nations named Czechoslovakia a victim of aggression. Molotov ridiculed the very idea. League involvement, he said, would "ensure the maximum of talk and the minimum of results." The Anglo-French might easily stand idly by while "Bolivia" blocked all action at Geneva. It was just one more nail in the coffin of Anglo-Soviet détente.[143]

In the end, Britain was left only with what Chamberlain called "menacing silence" to deter Hitler in Poland, hoping the Polish guarantee would not have to be honoured, that somehow Hitler would restrain himself—a forlorn hope once the Soviet pact had been signed.[144]

Behind the scenes, Molotov was racing ahead, and Berlin would send him no low-level negotiator. On 14 August, Foreign Minister von Ribbentrop proposed himself to Moscow, to open a "new future" and settle "every issue from the Baltic to the Black Sea"—almost the same offer the Soviets had made to the Anglo-French a few months earlier. Just before midnight on August 21st...

Berlin radio interrupted a musical programme with a triumphant announcement. Ribbentrop was going to Moscow to conclude a non-aggression pact. For most Europeans it was a message of misery: war was coming. For Hitler the neutrality and economic assistance of the Soviet Union made it possible to risk a second world war.[145]

Back in London, enjoying the comforts of his Victorian study, Ivan Maisky pondered the end of the "new" Triple Entente. Ignored by Moscow, he remained a friendly interlocutor with the British, meeting cordially with Anthony Eden, with the war already a month old. It was regrettable, he told Eden, that Halifax had refused to visit Moscow; if he had, things might be better now.

Eden responded that given what had happened, it may have been for the best. On the contrary, Maisky retorted, "if the visit had taken place, the position would have been different."

73

As for Poland (by then dissected and partitioned between Hitler and Stalin) and the Baltic States (all but occupied, with pro-Soviet "elections" planned for 1940), Maisky said it was only natural for Russia "that certain vital strategic points should be under control." The USSR "had not been grasping. The Soviet frontier with Poland even now included less territory than Czarist Russia had held."[146]

Churchill's Favourable Reference

Hitler had long worried over possible *rapprochement* between Germany's old World War I adversaries. "You need never fear Britain," Ribbentrop had assured him, "until you hear her talking of Russia as an ally. Then it means she is really going to war."[147] Stalin, supreme after purging his potential enemies, was open to expansion or influence in Czarist lands that had won independence after Versailles—thus the freedom of action he demanded on his western border in *any* pact, either with the Anglo-French *or* Hitler. Chamberlain was unwilling to contemplate a Soviet treaty of that nature (or probably any nature). Hitler was not.

Churchill, a private Member of Parliament without office, was able to play only a background role as Britain considered a Russian arrangement. But it is incorrect to believe he did not call for one until 1938.[148] He had many conversations with principals, including Nazis, which he duly forwarded to the Foreign Office.[149] On Conservative back benches, his influence grew as the situation worsened.

Up until Munich, Churchill's stand on Russia was closer to that of his party than has been generally recognized.[150] After Munich, he correctly concluded that the only way left to prevent war was to revive the Triple Entente that had faced Germany in World War I. In view of Stalin's obvious ambitions in eastern Europe, the question is whether that alone would have prevented a world conflagration: an issue we shall now consider.

Chapter 7

Lost Best Hope:
The America Factor, 1918-39

"America should have minded her own business and stayed out of the World War. If you hadn't entered the war the Allies would have made peace with Germany in the Spring of 1917. Had we made peace then there would have been no collapse in Russia followed by Communism, no breakdown in Italy followed by Fascism, and Germany would not have signed the Versailles Treaty, which has enthroned Nazism in Germany....it would have saved over one million British, French, American, and other lives."

—Alleged statement by Churchill, August 1936

Churchill, celebrating Thanksgiving Day, 23 November 1944, spoke of an all-powerful destiny which brought Britain and America together. (AP wirephoto)

Google the words at the top of this page and you will find at least a half dozen Internet citations attributing them to Winston Churchill—an intriguing way to consider his views on America's role in the world, which are vital to understanding his strategies in the late 1930s.[151]

The Great War of 1914-18, born of nationalism and entangled alliances, at first tempted few Americans to participate. Churchill understood this.[152] But on America's entry into the war in April 1917, he was unequivocal: "There is no need to exaggerate the material assistance [but] the moral consequence of the United States joining the Allies was indeed the deciding cause in the conflict...."[153] Without America, World War I "would have ended in a peace by negotiation, or, in other words, a German victory."[153]

Griffin and the *Enquirer*

In 1926 William S. Griffin (1898-1949), a protégé of Churchill's publisher friend William Randolph Hearst, founded the *New York Enquirer*, a Sunday platform for ideas which Hearst might adopt in his own newspapers.[154] Hearst and Griffin had opposed American entry into World War I; both were isolationists in the 1930s.

In 1942, with America at war again, a grand jury indicted the unrepentant Griffin for sedition, though the charges were later dropped.[155] Griffin died in 1949; the *Enquirer*'s circulation was only 17,000 when it was sold in 1952 to Generoso Pope, Jr., who renamed it the *National Enquirer,* the supermarket tabloid it remains to this day.[156]

Griffin's allegation that Churchill wished America to "mind its own business" remains the strongest claim that Churchill opposed U.S. involvement in Europe. By examining Churchill's reaction, we may learn what he really thought.

They began with a meeting Griffin had with Churchill in London on 5 August 1936. He had asked for the visit as a newspaperman with "no axe to grind."[157] Clearly this was a dodge. No sooner had they met than he asked Churchill when Britain was going to pay her war debts.

Churchill snorted. World War I debts, he believed, were the main sticking point between Britain and America. They led, he said, to a vicious circle: America loaned money to Germany, which used it to pay Britain and France reparations, which Britain and France used to pay debts to America.

In 1932, reacting to the possibility that Germany's economy would collapse in the Depression, the Lausanne Conference ended German reparations, but not war debts owed the U.S. by France and Britain. The only commonality between war debts and reparations is that they are both about money, but one depended on the other. Churchill wrote: "If Germany does not pay, France and Italy will not pay what they owe either to Great Britain or to the United States. Thus it all comes back to England...the question is: 'How much will England pay?'"[158]

According to Griffin, Churchill responded to the debt question by saying Britain should "deduct fifty percent of the cost of all the shot and shell she fired at the Germans from the time America declared war in the Spring of 1917 until she actually put troops in the front lines a year later," an estimated $4.9 billion. "There was no one in England happier" than he over America's entry into the late war, Churchill allegedly continued, but he "could see now that [U.S.] entry had been a great mistake." Yet of the next war Churchill said: "You may want to stay out [but] you will find yourselves fighting shoulder to shoulder with us."[159]

As war threatened in the summer of 1939, Churchill's alleged comments were repeated in the U.S. Congress by isolationist Senator Robert Rice Reynolds (D., N.C.) who said he had them from Griffin personally. Angrily denying he had said any such thing, Churchill engaged an attorney, William N. Stokes, Jr. of Houston, who remonstrated with Reynolds, to no avail.[160]

Churchill's next embarrassment was an August 26th German radio broadcast quoting his supposed remarks. When *The New York Times* asked him to confirm, Churchill pronounced the story "a vicious lie."[161] Griffin responded with a $1 million libel suit, asking New York courts to attach Churchill's earnings from his New York publishers against the settlement.[162]

Churchill denied having said "anything which remotely resembles in substance or form the passage [Griffin claims]. These views are entirely contrary to all the views I hold and have frequently expressed." Griffin, he continued, had "exploited a private conversation," but this might have been allowed to pass if his story had not been "the exact opposite of the truth, and a palpable travesty and distortion of anything I have ever said or thought."[163]

The case dragged on until 22 October 1942, when a New York judge dismissed Griffin's lawsuit, apparently because Griffin had not appeared in court. Suffering from the effects of a heart attack, he was still under indictment for sedition, and was under house arrest in the hospital.[164]

Churchill's View of the American Relationship

The incident is significant less for Griffin's claim than for Churchill's denial, and true opinion. Germany, Churchill had written, had calculated that its U-boats could starve Britain before America's intervention proved decisive. But the Royal Navy had defeated the U-boats, assuring "that the war could be carried on until the power of the United States could, if necessary, be fully exerted on the battlefields of Europe."[165]

One historical event does not cause the next one. Nazism was *not* the inevitable consequence of Germany's defeat—except insofar as any defeated nation hopes for a strong leader, and Germany found that leader in Hitler. The real reasons for Hitler's rise, Churchill believed, were the harsh peace of Versailles and Germany's post-war economic recession.[166]

A weakened Kaiser in post-war Germany would have given in to Hitler as easily as President von Hindenburg. The exiled Kaiser held his nose (or pretended to) over Hitler's pogroms, but was himself anti-Semitic, and congratulated Hitler on his 1940 victories. Hitler held Wilhelm in contempt, having concluded he didn't need him.[167] Nor would a 1917 German victory have forestalled fascism in Italy or communism in Russia.

In reality, Churchill considered the United States vital in both World Wars. More than that, in the early Thirties, he had argued for something very close to a common currency, wishing "to see the reduction in the gold content of the dollar taken as part of a bargain with Great Britain, so that all the prestige of the two great financial countries could be enlisted behind the new unit of values."[168]

When James Roosevelt visited Chartwell on 8 October 1933, Churchill took a sheet of paper and drew an intertwined pound and dollar sign, which he referred to as the "Sterling Dollar....Pray bear this to your father from me," he told President Roosevelt's son. "Tell him this must be the currency of the future." What if, James replied, his father preferred to call it the "Dollar Sterling"? Churchill beamed: "It is all the same."[169]

Roosevelt's Proffered Hand

Churchill made his views about America known as early as the 1935 general election: "We must keep in the closest touch with the United States of America, whose navy is as important to the peace of the world as our own."[170] Two years later, Churchill was heartened to hear of President Roosevelt's "Quarantine Speech" in Chicago. "A reign of terror and international lawlessness," FDR said, threatened "the very foundations of civilization." The President proposed economic pressure on the aggressor nations: "When an epidemic of physical disease starts to spread, the community approves and joins in a quarantine of the patients in order to protect the health of the community against the spread of the disease."[171] Churchill reacted instantly. Roosevelt's speech, he said,

...expressed in eloquent language exactly the same ideas that are in our minds, and I have no doubt that it will be cordially welcomed by Mr. Chamberlain....an understanding so perfect and spontaneous between two branches of the English-speaking race is bound to bring an enormous contribution and consolidation of those forces in the world which stand for peace and freedom.[172]

A fortnight later, Churchill addressed the question of imposing sanctions, in this instance on Japan: "In this matter there is one single rule. We must act in support of the United States....If our two countries go together in this matter, I doubt whether any harm could come to either of us."[173] This was redolent of his constant theme as Prime

Minister in later years: "If we are together nothing is impossible. If we are divided all will fail."[174]

Neville Chamberlain's opportunity to welcome Roosevelt's support of the democracies arrived on 11 January 1938, when the President sent him a secret message. Paralleling his remarks to Congress the week before, Roosevelt expressed his concern over the international situation and proposed to invite representatives of Germany, Britain, France and Italy to Washington in the hopes of finding an easement of their affairs, or at least taking part in such a meeting. Before doing so, he wrote, he wished to consult with the Chamberlain government.

It was a golden opportunity, but Chamberlain was in a belligerent mood. In December, after Japan attacked British and American gunboats on the Yangtze, he had proposed a concerted Anglo-American response including a joint naval task force; Roosevelt had settled for a Japanese apology. The Americans, Chamberlain complained, "are incredibly slow and have missed innumerable busses....I do wish the Japs would beat up an American or two!"[175] His wish would be fulfilled four years later at Pearl Harbor.

Chamberlain's impatience with Roosevelt was fanned by his close adviser Sir Horace Wilson, who dismissed the President's initiative as "woolly rubbish."[176] Without consulting Eden or the Foreign Office, Chamberlain replied, asking Roosevelt to consider whether his efforts "might not cut across" concurrent British efforts to placate the dictators, including possible British recognition of Mussolini's occupation of Abyssinia—a possibility Roosevelt greeted with revulsion. FDR's answer conveyed his disappointment. "Before you get this," Horace Wilson wrote a colleague, "Roosevelt may have obscured the horizon by another cloud of words, but it should clear off after a bit."[177]

Chamberlain's rebuff of Roosevelt ended the last frail chance to save the world from catastrophe. Churchill was on holiday in the South of France during this episode, and could not have known of it at the time. His memoirs were censorious:

That Mr. Chamberlain, with his limited outlook and inexperience of the European scene, should have possessed the self-sufficiency to wave away the proffered hand stretched out across the Atlantic leaves one, even at this date, breathless with amazement. The lack of all sense of proportion, and even of self-preservation, which this episode reveals in an upright, competent, well-meaning man, charged with the destinies of our country and all who depended upon it, is appalling. One cannot today even reconstruct the state of mind which would render such gestures possible.[178]

"The Price of Greatness is Responsibility"

There was a sequel to Roosevelt's proffer—too late, World War II having already begun, but nonetheless welcome. It was heavy with portent. On 11 September 1939, the President wrote to Churchill, now First Lord of the Admiralty (and pointedly not to Chamberlain):

My dear Mr. Churchill, It is because you and I occupied similar positions in the World War that I want you to know how glad I am that you are back again in the Admiralty. Your problems are, I realize, complicated by new factors but the essential is not very different. What I want you and the Prime Minister to know is that I shall at all times welcome it if you will keep me in touch personally with anything you want me to know about. You can always send sealed letters through your pouch or my pouch.[179]

After securing Chamberlain's approval, Churchill "responded with alacrity," signing himself "Naval Person": the beginning, he said, of "a long and memorable correspondence…lasting till [FDR's] death more than five years later."[180] To that letter we may trace the beginning of what would become the Anglo-American "special relationship."

Four years later, much had happened. The relationship had borne considerable fruit, and Churchill, speaking at Harvard, was able to embody all of his feeling and trust in what he often called "the Great Republic":

It is said that the League of Nations failed. If so, that is largely because it was abandoned, and later on betrayed: because those who were its best friends were till a very late period infected with a futile pacifism: because the United States, the originating impulse, fell out of the line….The price of greatness is responsibility…but one cannot rise to be in many ways the leading community in the civilised world without being involved in its problems, without being convulsed by its agonies and inspired by its causes…. There is no halting-place at this point. We have now reached a stage in the journey where there can be no pause. We must go on. It must be world anarchy or world order.[181]

Chapter 8
Was World War II Preventable?
"Embalm, cremate and bury—take no risks!"

"President Roosevelt one day asked what this War should be called. My answer was, 'The Unnecessary War.' If the United States had taken an active part in the League of Nations, and if the League of Nations had been prepared to use concerted force, even had it only been European force, to prevent the rearmament of Germany, there was no need for further serious bloodshed."
—Churchill, Brussels, 16 November 1945

Churchill's post-war theme—at Fulton (above), Brussels, The Hague and Zurich—was peace through strength, preparedness and alliance. (Missouri Archives)

66 Those who are prone by temperament and character to seek sharp and clear-cut solutions of difficult and obscure problems, who are ready to fight whenever some challenge comes from a foreign Power, have not always been right," Churchill

wrote.[182] We should not deprecate good and honest leaders whose opinions impelled them to actions which in hindsight proved mistaken. We can best judge history in the light of situations as they appeared at the time, not through facts then unknown, and the advantage of hindsight.

Nor may we, in judging whether World War II was preventable, base our conclusions on a single Churchill prescription. As Williamson Murray wrote, "too many historians possess linear minds, and seem to believe that were one historical event changed, everything else would remain the same."[183]

Germany Arming (Chapter 1)

Had Churchill's early warnings about Germany found support, Britain would have remained militarily superior. "Hitler fired the starting-gun in February 1933," wrote R.A.C. Parker, but "only the Germans moved." It wasn't until mid-1934 that Britain began a small rearmament programme, and not until 1936 that the Cabinet began to think the country might have to fight. The stark dichotomy in forces is shown by Parker's figures for aircraft production that year: 5112 for Germany, 1877 for Britain.[184]

Churchill's words on Hitler were not expressions of admiration, except in the narrow sense of Hitler's political success. While hoping for the best, Churchill was under no illusions. He could not have predicted Hitler's timing and strategy, though he was right about Hitler's targets.

Was Churchill's relative silence over Mussolini's invasion of Abyssinia in October 1935 inconsistency or realism? Italy's aggression, unlike Hitler's, was directed far from pivotal Europe. Similar reasoning made Churchill consider Germany more dangerous than Russia, which until 1939 had made no aggressive moves beyond its borders—a judgment for which he was later criticised by anti-communists.

If Churchill was right that Hitler was the central threat to peace, how might the British government have acted to heed him? Should it have imposed, say, sanctions against Germany for rearming, or occupying the Rhineland? Would that have changed anything?

Churchill *at the time* argued that Britain should abandon disarmament. Remarkably, the policies he deplored survive today, despite all we have learned. Recently, a U.S. State Department official said that America had remained safe in the nuclear age not because of her nuclear arsenal, but because of an intricate system of treaties, laws and agreements. The 1920s and 1930s were replete with treaties, laws and agreements.

Churchill favoured collective security, provided it was backed with solid agreements and real strength. Without them, collective security was a fraud, "a disastrous means of deceiving well-meaning pacific communities into putting themselves at the mercy of predatory Governments. There is not much collective security in a flock of sheep on the way to the butcher."[185]

Germany Armed (Chapter 2)

Neither Baldwin (1935-37) nor Chamberlin (1937-40) were against rearming, but Churchill wanted more of it, sooner. Churchill admitted that "It has given me pain to record these disagreements with so many men who I liked

87

or respected...."[186] But he had to disagree with them, because they were wrong.

The Gathering Storm is a great read—it certainly hooked me—but it cannot be read innocently. An example, which incidentally teaches us much about the Churchill persona, is a damning entry in the index under Baldwin: "...confesses to putting party before country."

This refers to a 12 November 1936 speech by Baldwin, referring to the 1933-34 period: "Supposing I had gone to the country and said that Germany was rearming and that we must rearm, does anybody think that this pacific democracy would have rallied to that cry at that moment? I cannot think of anything that would have made the loss of the election from my point of view more certain."[187]

The next day Churchill wrote a friend: "I have never heard such a squalid confession from a public man as Baldwin offered us yesterday."[188] For Baldwin "to avow that he had not done his duty in regard to national safety because he was afraid of losing the election," he wrote in *The Gathering Storm,* amounted to "indecency."[189]

Some historians say Churchill did Baldwin an injustice.[190] In both *The Gathering Storm* and his 1938 speech volume, *Arms and the Covenant,*[191] he quoted Baldwin selectively, implying that Baldwin was referring to the actual election in November 1935, when in fact Baldwin meant a hypothetical election in 1933-34. Indeed, on 12 November 1936 Churchill had spoken before Baldwin, saying that the Prime Minister *had* campaigned in 1935 on rearming.

It is not a pleasant story and nothing can change it. Churchill or his editor (in 1938 this was his son Randolph) edited Baldwin's defence of himself. Among key omissions was Baldwin's statement that the election gave him "a mandate for doing a thing [rearming] that no one, twelve months before, would have believed possible...had I taken such action as my Rt Hon Friend [Churchill] desired me to take, it would have defeated entirely the end I had in view."[192]

But Baldwin is not entirely exonerated. To appreciate this, one must read the *entire* passage from Churchill's 12 November 1935 speech, which *also* doesn't appear in *The Gathering Storm*. While Baldwin had "fought and largely won" the 1935 election on rearmament, Churchill declared,

... it was very difficult to see what he really intended, because...he also made the statement: "I give you my word there will be no great armaments....There has not been, there is not, and there will not be any question of huge armaments or materially increased forces." Frankly, I do not understand what that could have meant, because an Air Force equal to the gigantic force being constructed in Germany would certainly involve a huge expenditure....[193]

Thus Baldwin not only admitted that, *had there been* a 1933-34 election, he would not have pushed for rearmament because he would have lost; he also gave mixed messages about how much he would rearm in the 1935 election campaign.

Churchill's ringing declaration the previous June stands in contrast to Baldwin's: "I would endure with patience the roar of exultation that would go up when I was proved wrong, because it would lift a load off my heart and off the hearts of many Members. What does it matter who gets exposed or discomfited? If the country is safe, who cares for individual politicians, in or out of office?"[194]

The difference in statecraft is very clear. 1) Baldwin wanted to rearm, and campaigned for it in the 1935 election; he won, and he did rearm. 2) But Baldwin was more reluctant about risking votes than Churchill, and was less urgent and ambitious than Churchill about rearming. 3) It would have been better in 1940 to have had more weapons; Churchill had consistently urged that they be provided.

Churchill wasn't always right, but on the big question of rearmament, his sense of urgency was palpable, his prescriptions undeniable. It is now the consensus that Britain should have started arming vigorously in 1935, and that doing so would have denied Hitler the superiority he gained. "We have never," Churchill said...

...been likely to get into trouble by having an extra thousand or two of up-to-date aeroplanes at our disposal. Starting as late as we did, we should have at once opened our own industry to the fullest compass and at the same time used our wealth to buy to the utmost extent abroad. As the man whose mother-in-law had died in Brazil replied, when asked how the remains should be disposed of, "Embalm, cremate and bury. Take no risks!"[195]

The Rhineland (Chapter 3)

Given Baldwin's need for public mandates, his handling of French Foreign Minister Flandin after Hitler had occupied the Rhineland was predictable. There was no possibility that Britain would mobilise, Baldwin told

Flandin; the British wanted peace. Churchill snorted at Baldwin's interpretation of his duty.

Baldwin's reaction may not be so crucial. Even with Baldwin's backing, would Flandin's call for action have been supported by the French cabinet? Resistance to war was at least as strong in Paris as in London. We cannot be sure that a more determined Britain would have carried the French. We know *now* that Hitler was prepared to retreat if France resisted, but the Western allies didn't know this *at the time.*

In his defence, Churchill *did* say more than Baldwin and other leaders about the implications of the Rhineland—as much as was politic for a private Member of Parliament without office. He did believe all-out war would not be necessary—and on Hitler's own evidence, he was right. This is not the same as advocating declaring war on Germany. By 1938, of course, the situation had worsened dramatically.

Austria (Chapter 4)

Churchill did not propose direct military action to stop the Austrian *Anschluss* in March 1938. Instead he advocated united opposition and collective security. The choice, he said, was...

...either to submit, like Austria, or else to take effective measures while time remains to ward off the danger and, if it cannot be warded off, to cope with it....[By 1940] the German Army "will certainly be much larger than the French Army....Why be edged and pushed farther down the slope in a disorderly expostulating crowd of embarrassed States? Why not make a stand while there is

91

still a good company of united, very powerful countries that share our dangers and aspirations?"[196]

After the war Churchill was more specific: "...the prospect of a mobilized Royal Navy and French Army, together with either Austria's eighteen divisions or the formidable Czech army dug in on their borders, might have given pause even to Hitler—who was only acting, as he admitted to Schuschnigg, because Britain and France would "not lift a finger."[197]

This is not admissible in our catalogue of Churchill's recommendations at the time. What *is* admissible is his stated need for collective security—which, like his other imprecations, was ignored.

Munich (Chapter 5)

The arguments against Churchill's proposals during the Czechoslovak crisis are threefold: (1) the British people were against military action; (2) Hitler was entrenched in power; and (3) Munich bought time for Britain to become stronger. These points are widely expressed and insightful, but not in the end dispositive.

(a) Public Attitudes: British *and* German

British public opinion had stiffened considerably since Hitler had absorbed the Rhineland and Austria. When he turned to Czechoslovakia, Britons were outraged. Lord Halifax, so often portrayed as a pacifist, led a cabinet revolt, saying Hitler could never be trusted again, telegraphing Chamberlain: "Great mass of public opinion seems to be hardening in sense of feeling that we have gone to the limit of concession."[198] In 1939, Britons largely supported declaring war over Poland, which was far less able to defend itself than Czechoslovakia.

Churchill's critique of his government's reluctance for a showdown in 1938 came only a month after Munich, when he declared his faith that Britons would accept reality, provided it was carefully explained to them:

I am convinced that with adequate leadership, democracy can be a more efficient form of government than Fascism. In this country at any rate the people can readily be convinced that it is necessary to make sacrifices, and they will willingly undertake them if the situation is put clearly and fairly before them. No one can doubt that it was within the power of the National Government at any time within the last seven years to rearm the country at any pace required without resistance from the mass of the people. The difficulty was that the leaders failed to appreciate the need and to warn the people, or were afraid to do their duty, not that the democratic system formed an impediment.[199]

While we often hear that Britons rejected military action in 1938, we rarely hear the counterpoint: that the Germans too had had a bellyful of war and its disastrous aftermath. Rapturous Germans, believing he was bringing peace, greeted Chamberlain in Bad Godesberg on 22 September 1938. Sullen Berliners watching Hitler's review of motorized columns five days later comprised, in the words of an eye-witness, "the most striking demonstration against war I've ever seen." Disgusted, Hitler remarked to Goebbels, "I can't lead a war with such people."[200]

(b) Hitler's Security—or Insecurity

The opportunity for Hitler's removal by a high-ranking cabal of plotters was greater in September 1938 than at any other time in his career. While Mr. Chamberlain compared the schemers to Jacobean recidivists in King William's time, Hitler took a more serious view of them. Of the twelve chief conspiracists, seven—Generals Beck and Witzleben, Admiral Canaris, Oster, Helldorf, Kleist and Dohnanyi—were executed for treason.

The cabal was actually ready to move when Chamberlain announced he was going to Munich. "Only one man could prevent Hitler's assassination and the forcible overthrow of his regime," said one recent writer. "That man was Neville Chamberlain."[201] Of course, that conclusion follows only if you accept the post-war claims of the plotters, and in Mr. Chamberlain's defence, you cannot make policy on the off-chance that a claque of disgruntled opponents are really going to act.

(c) Relative Readiness

We have seen how underwhelming Hitler's fighting forces appeared in 1938, during the occupation of Austria and before Munich. The question is: If fighting or resisting Hitler in 1938 was so ludicrous, what was there about fighting him in 1939-40 that made it preferable? Was it the eradication of Poland in three weeks, the Low Countries in sixteen days, France in six weeks? Whether Churchill was right at every juncture in the 1930s is debatable, but over Czechoslovakia, the evidence that he was right is powerful:

There is no merit in putting off a war for a year if, when it comes, it is a far worse war or one much harder to win....For the French Government to leave her faithful ally Czechoslovakia to her fate was a melancholy lapse from which flowed terrible consequences. Not only wise and fair policy, but chivalry, honour, and sympathy for a small threatened people made an overwhelming concentration. Great Britain, who would certainly have fought if bound by treaty obligations, was nevertheless now deeply involved, and it must be recorded with regret that the British Government not only acquiesced but encouraged the French Government in a fatal course. [202]

Russia (Chapter 7)

By 1939 the chances of saving the world from the Second World War had narrowed appreciably. British official policy, contrary to its many critics, did not give Germany everything it wanted; it strove to prevent German dominance in Europe. Britain's leaders hoped for a prosperous and peaceful Reich, a trading partner, a buffer against Bolshevism, and would have granted Germany a leading interest in eastern Europe. But Hitler wanted more, as R.A.C. Parker wrote:

He had in mind the creation of a powerful German empire militarily unbeatable by any possible combination of adversaries. To this the British government and the majority of the British people would not voluntarily assent. That made conciliatory efforts pointless. Nor did British policy deter. It is probable that Chamberlain encouraged

Germans, who might otherwise have restrained Hitler, to believe that British threats to resist German aggression were empty.[203]

The Soviets had been left out by the Western allies at every diplomatic juncture, and only relatively minor British functionaries were sent to Moscow, by sea, to discuss mutual collaboration in 1939. The Russians concluded, Parker wrote, that Britain "aimed for a bargain with Hitler at the expense of the Soviet Union."[204]

Parker denies that Chamberlain aimed for a deal at Soviet expense, but given Maisky's comments *at the time,* one can understand Soviet suspicions. Hard heads like Molotov and Stalin had watched as Germany received concession after concession at the expense of the French, Austrians and Czechs. Why should they conclude that the Anglo-French would prove reliable? Chamberlain stoutly resisted Churchill's call for a Franco-British alliance with Russia, and it was a cardinal principle among many Chamberlain supporters that Germany was the bulwark against a Bolshevised Europe.

Churchill's calls for a Russian pact or understanding stood no chance with the British government, because the Soviet price was a free hand in eastern Europe. Cynics might say in hindsight, why not give it to them? Why fight a bloody six-year war to end up with the same situation: a potent tyranny dominating eastern Europe, and a protracted Cold War?

Would Churchill's proposed Anglo-Soviet-French mutual defence arrangement have made war unnecessary? Not in the end. It would have left both devils still standing—for a time. And then what? Absent a widened war, with accelerated U.S. nuclear research, would Hitler's early experiments with "heavy water" have led him to the atom bomb before anyone else? We don't know.

America (Chapter 7)

Contrary to isolationists like William Griffin, Churchill consistently believed that America should be involved in the world. To have rejected President Roosevelt's "proffered hand stretched out across the Atlantic," he wrote later, "leaves one, even at this date, breathless with amazement."[205] Clearly he felt the same way at the time.

Of course he was right. Would a more favourable response to Roosevelt's offer of American involvement, even if only as a mediator, have prevented war? This we cannot know. We *do* know that Hitler occasionally hesitated when contemplating the forces likely arrayed against him. Recall that on 27 September 1938, when Britain mobilised the fleet, Hitler said "the English fleet might shoot after all," and postponed German mobilisation.[206]

Changing one historical event does not mean subsequent events would remain the same. The United States in 1938 remained opposed to involvement in what it saw as another European quarrel. Roosevelt, let alone Congress, which had the sole authority to declare war, was in no position overtly to support the Anglo-French. It is possible that Roosevelt as a mediator might have felt obliged to take no side in the seemingly intractable conflict between Hitler's ambitions and the Western democracies.

Nevertheless, Churchill's position on America made sense. No one can know what Roosevelt's involvement would have led to—but it would certainly have changed the international equation, for the first time since 1918. It seems reasonable to consider that Roosevelt's devotion to democracy would have inclined him to support, or at least encourage, the Anglo-French. It would have hurt nothing to find out. There were no other possible allies on the horizon in those days save Soviet Russia—with whom Chamberlain was determined not to treat.

Summary:
What Churchill Teaches us Today

Chicago Tribune, January 1965

From the time he was a young man, Churchill feared and warned against modern scientific war, and did what he could—despite the prevailing inaccurate view of him as a war enthusiast—to prevent it. "History with its flickering lamp stumbles along the trail of the past," he said, "trying to reconstruct its scenes, to revive its echoes, and kindle with pale gleams the passion of former days."[207] We have seen how Churchill approached the climacterics of the 1930s, and considered whether he was right—with a degree of conjecture, since we cannot know the outcome had this or that option been tried. The reader may judge if the war was preventable. For me the answer is "yes, but with great difficulty."

Churchill's critique began with the assertion that if Britain's leaders had frankly engaged the British public with the facts and rearmed faster, saner elements in Germany would have prevailed, in time, supplanting Hitler. If, it continues, the Americans or more likely the Russians had joined "a formidable array of peace-defending powers," Hitler would have recoiled.

Among the crises of the 1930s, one stands out as an opportunity to avoid global war. The Munich agreement in September 1938 made Hitler stronger, removed the threat of a coup, bucked up German public sentiment, and vouchsafed Germany the armaments of Czechoslovakia. Churchill maintained that if, before Munich,

...Great Britain, France and Russia had jointly declared that they would act together upon Nazi Germany if Herr Hitler committed an act of unprovoked aggression against this small State, and if they had told Poland, Yugoslavia and Rumania what they meant to do in good time, and invited them to join the combination of peace-defending Powers...the German Dictator would have been confronted with such a formidable array, that he would have been deterred from his purpose.[208]

Churchill's other prescriptions during those Lost Years are less clear. His voice was muted over the Rhineland and Austria, unheard over the overtures of Roosevelt. His advice about Russia was ignored, perhaps for good reason—one could argue that Chamberlain's appreciation of Stalin's ultimate ambitions was more accurate than Churchill's.

One cannot help reflecting, however, that Churchill was right on the big issues, like Hitler and disarmament, and with his military background and experience, would have been less likely than his predecessors to be bamboozled by a clever and resourceful enemy. Under Churchill, closer attention would have been paid to preparedness. The sad story of Churchill in those fateful years reminds us once again, if we have to be reminded, of a maxim by someone other than he, that the price of liberty is eternal vigilance.

Endnotes

Chapter 1

1. Adolf Hitler, *Mein Kampf*, 2 vols., (Berlin: Eher Verlaf, 1925-26). An abridged English edition was first published by Hurst & Blackett, London, on 13 October 1933, though excerpts appeared in *The Times* during July.

2. Wilhelm Cuno (1876-1933), German treasury official 1907-16, Food Controller 1917-18, Chancellor November 1922-August 1923; Chairman and General Manager, Hamburg-Amerika Line, 1918-33.

3. Hamilton to Churchill, 24 October 1930, in Martin Gilbert, ed., *Winston S. Churchill* (hereinafter *WSC*), Document Volume 12 (Hillsdale, Michigan: Hillsdale College Press, 2009), 208-09 (Churchill papers: 8/269). In the 14 September German election the National Socialists received 6.4 million votes (18%), taking 107 seats, second highest in the Reichstag. The Social Democrats won 143 seats, the Communists 77, the Centre Party 68.

4. Churchill, "Reparations Abandoned," House of Commons, 11 July 1932 in *Winston S. Churchill: His Complete Speeches 1897-1953* (hereinafter *CS*), 8 vols. (New York Bowker, 1974) V 5193-94.

5. Ibid.

6. Winston S. Churchill, *The Gathering Storm* (London: Cassell, 1948), 65.

7. Ernst Hanfstaengl, *Hitler—The Missing Years* (London: Eyre & Spottiswoode, 1957), 184. Richard M. Langworth, ed., *Churchill in His Own Words* (hereinafter *CIHOW*, London: Ebury Press, 2012), 12.

8. *CIHOW,* 19.

9. *Gathering Storm*, 65-66.

10. Franz von Papen (1879-1969), German Chancellor June-November 1932, Ambassador to Austria 1934-38 (where paved the way for the 1938 *Anschluss*); and to Turkey (1939-44. Acquitted of war crimes at Nuremberg, he served a year in prison, was released, and rehabilitated himself as an author and champion of European unity.

11. *WSC,* Doc. Vol. 12, 477 n. 1.

12. Churchill, House of Commons, 13 April 1933, *CS* V 5263.

13. Ibid.

14. Churchill, House of Commons, 7 February 1934, *CIHOW,* 247.

15. Churchill, House of Commons, 13 March 1934, *CIHOW,* 247.

16. Churchill, House of Commons, 13 July 1934, *CIHOW,* 248.

17. Ibid.

18. *WSC,* Doc. Vol. 12, 923.

19. Churchill, debate on German rearmament, House of Commons, 28 November 1934, in *CIHOW,* 237.

20. Orme Garton Sargent (1884-1962). Entered Foreign Office, 1906, Head of the Central Department of the Foreign Office, 1928-33; Assistant Under-Secretary of State for Foreign Affairs, 1933. Knighted, 1937. Deputy Under-Secretary of State, 1939; Permanent Under-Secretary, 1946-49.

21. Sargent to Churchill, 13 November 1934. *WSC,* Doc. Vol. 12, 920 (Churchill Papers, CHAR 2/229).

Chapter 2

22. Churchill to his wife, "Chartwell Bulletin No. 8," 8 March 1935, *WSC,* Doc. Vol. 12, 1107.

23. Rt Hon John Simon, First Viscount Simon (1873-1954), Foreign Secretary 1931-35, Chancellor of the Exchequer 1937-40. A friend and contemporary of Churchill's, he held numerous Cabinet posts in both World Wars, ending the second as Lord Chancellor in the Churchill government.

24. Churchill, "Air Estimates," House of Commons, 19 March 1935, *CIHOW*, 249.

25. Churchill, *Gathering Storm*, 96.

26. *WSC*, Doc. Vol. 12, 1145, note 1: "According to the Air Ministry's calculations Britain's existing first-line Home strength in the air was no more than 453 aircraft. More than 230 of the aeroplanes which Simon told Hitler were Britain's first-line strength were, in fact, Fleet Air Arm and Auxiliary Units. Of the former, amounting to 110 aircraft, 'there is no assurance that they would even be in home waters in an emergency,' while the 127 Auxiliary Units 'correspond to "Territorial" and not to regular forces.' This figure of 453 first-line aircraft corresponded with the Air Ministry figure of 850 German first-line and 'Immediate Reserve' aircraft for February 1935."

27. Churchill to his wife, "Chartwell Bulletin No. 10," 5 April 1935, *WSC*, Doc. Vol. 12, 1145. Air Ministry figures, Martin Gilbert noted, "bore out the fears which had been expressed in the Foreign Office by Sir John Simon" and others.

28. Harold Sidney Harmsworth, First Viscount Rothermere (1868-1940). Newspaper magnate and developer of the *Daily Mail* and *Daily Mirror*. While favouring British rearmament, his newspapers singularly advocated an Anglo-German alliance. He was still congratulating Hitler in 1939; nearing death as the war broke out, he finally reconsidered.

29. Hitler to Rothermere, Berlin, 3 May 1935. Churchill Papers, CHAR 2/235/79-86.

30. Churchill to Rothermere 12 May 1935, in *WSC, Doc.* Vol. 12, 1169-70.

31. Rothermere to Churchill, 13 May 1935, ibid., 1171-72.

32. Ibid.

33. Reeves Shaw to Churchill, 15 May 1935, *WSC, Doc.* Vol. 12, 1175.

34. Winston S. Churchill, "Hitler and His Choice," in *Great Contemporaries* (London: Thornton Butterworth, 1937). Quoted from the 1990 edition (London: Leo Cooper), 165-72.

35. Martin Gilbert, *Churchill: A Life* (London: Heinemann, 1991), 580-81.

36. Winston S. Churchill, "This Age of Government by Great Dictators," *Collected Essays* IV 397.

37. Winston S. Churchill, "Friendship with Germany," *Evening Standard*, 17 September 1937, in *Step by Step* (London: Odhams, 1947), 156.

38. Ibid.

39. Churchill to Lord Londonderry, 23 October 1937, in Gilbert, *Churchill: A Life*, 581.

40. Ibid., 581.

41. Churchill, 11 July 1935, *CS* VI 5653-56, *Parliamentary Debates* CCCIV 540-50. Richard Howard Powers, "Winston Churchill's Parliamentary Commentary on British Foreign Policy, 1935-1938" (hereinafter Powers, "Churchill's Commentary"), *The Journal of Modern History* 26:2, June 1954, 179.

42. *CS* VI 5663. For an accusation of misleading readers in his war memoirs see Powers, 179-80. See also the Preface to this book.

43. Churchill, House of Commons, 26 March 1936, *CS* VI 5717; and 20 July 1936, *CIHOW,* 493.

Chapter 3

44. Langworth, *CIHOW,* 438.

45. Ian Kershaw, *Hitler 1889-1936: Hubris* (New York: W.W. Norton, 1999), 588.

46. Manfred Weidhorn: "Churchill would have called Hitler's bluff, but he was in no position to do so. All he could do was virtually to shriek in the press, concerning the 'hideous drift' to war, 'Stop it! Stop it! Stop it now!'" Sir Robert Rhodes James: "Churchill said nothing about the Rhineland—nothing at all. He was hoping for Cabinet office and he kept quiet." Transcripts, "Churchill as Peacemaker," a symposium at the Woodrow Wilson Center for Scholars, Washington, D.C., 29 October 1994.

47. Churchill to his wife, 17 January 1936, in Martin Gilbert, ed., *WSC,* Doc. Vol. 13, *The Coming of War 1936-1939* (Hillsdale, Mich.: Hillsdale College Press, 2009), 15-16.

48. Joachim von Ribbentrop (1893-1946). German Ambassador to Britain, 1936-38, Foreign Minister, 1938-45. He played key roles in negotiating the 1935 Anglo-German Naval Treaty, the Anti-Comintern Pact with Japan, and the non-aggression pact with Soviet Russia in 1939. Convicted of war crimes at Nuremberg, he was hanged on 16 October 1946.

49. Michael Bloch, *Ribbentrop* (New York: Crown, 1993), 84.

50. Hitler, quoted in Anthony Eden, *Facing the Dictators* (London: Cassell, 1962), 339.

51. Anthony Eden, First Earl of Avon (1897-1977). Member of Parliament 1923-57, Foreign Secretary 1935-

38, 1940-45, 1951-55 Prime Minister 1955-57. Generally advocating a firm line toward Germany, he would resign from the Chamberlain government in 1938 over Britain's rebuff of Roosevelt's offer to mediate a peace conference and Chamberlain's overtures to Mussolini (see Chapter IV).

52. Maurice Gustave Gamelin (1872-1958). French general, headed French Army general staff from 1931 through 17 May 1940, when he was cashiered as France broke before the invading Nazis. In his defence, he had tried to cope with continuous cuts in Army funding before the war. An aide to General Joffre in World War I, was highly regarded, even by the Germans.

53. William Manchester, *The Last Lion,* Vol. 2, *Alone 1932-1940* (Boston: Little Brown, 1988), 581.

54. A.J.P. Taylor, *English History 1914-1945* (Oxford: Oxford University Press, 1970), 387-88.

55. Pierre Étienne Flandin (1889-1958). French Conservative, Prime Minister 1934-35, 1940-41, Foreign Minister when Hitler occupied the Rhineland. An admirer of Churchill, he hoped to secure British support over the Rhineland, which did not materialize.

56. Churchill, *Gathering Storm,* 152.

57. Keith Middlemas & John Barnes, *Baldwin: A Biography* (New York: Macmillan, 1969), 919.

58. Ibid., 919-20.

59. Maurice Ashley, *Churchill as Historian* (London: Secker & Warburg, 1968, 163-64.

60. Ronald Tree, *When the Moon was High* (London: Macmillan, 1974) 64-65.

61. Robert Rhodes James, *Churchill: A Study in Failure 1909-1939* (London: Weidenfeld & Nicolson, 1970), 262-63.

62. Gilbert, *Churchill: A Life,* 552.

63. Rhodes James, *Study in Failure,* 262-63

64. Churchill, *Gathering Storm,* 157

65. Churchill, Jewellers Association dinner, Birmingham, 14 March 1936, *CS* VI 5704-05.

66. Winston S. Churchill, *Arms and the Covenant* (London: Harrap, 1938), 301.

67. Winston S. Churchill, "Stop it Now!," *Evening Standard,* 3 April 1936, reprinted in *Step by Step* (London: Thornton Butterworth, 1939), 19.

68. Churchill to *The Times,* London, 20 April 1936, in Gilbert, *WSC,* Doc. Vol. 13, 101.

69. Robert Boothby, *Recollections of a Rebel* (London: Hutchinson, 1978), 93.

70. See for example Henry Pelling, *Winston Churchill, rev. ed.* (Ware, Dorset: Wordsworth, 1999), 375.

71. John Charmley, *Churchill: The End of Glory* (London: Hodder & Stoughton, 1993), 307.

72. Churchill, *Arms and the Covenant,* 101-02.

73. John Charmley, *Chamberlain and the Lost Peace* (London: John Curtis, 1989), xiii: "The lack of concerted response from the Versailles Powers revealed what was already apparent, that where the threat of defeat had brought unity, the reality of peace had engendered disunion."

74. Sir Robert Rhodes James to the author, 15 November 1994.

75. Sir Robert Rhodes James to the author, 24 May 1995.

76. Churchill complimented Mussolini at a 1927 press conference in Rome, where he had hoped to collect the Italian war debt; at several times in the 1930s; and in

an appeal to Mussolini not to turn on the collapsing Allies in 1940. It was only after Mussolini had declared war that he went from "greatest law-giver" to "whipped jackal" in the Churchill lexicon. Langworth, *CIHOW*, 169-70, 364-65.

Chapter 4

77. Charmley, *Chamberlain and the Lost Peace*, xii-xiii and correspondence with the author, 3 February 2015. Later plebiscites in the border provinces of Tyrol and Salzburg yielded majorities of 98% and 99% in favour of a unification with Germany. See S. W. Gould, "Austrian Attitudes toward Anschluss: October 1918-September 1919," *Journal of Modern History* 22 (3): 220-31.

78. See for example James W. Muller, "The Aftermath of the Great War," in J.W. Muller, ed., *Churchill as Peacemaker* (Cambridge: Cambridge University Press, 1997), 228-29. Muller described post-Versailles Austria as a "derelict state."

79. Martin Gilbert, *WSC*, Bio. Vol. 5, *The Prophet of Truth 1922-1939* (2009), 408-09.

80. Langworth, *CIHOW*, 204.

81. Richard Lamb, *The Drift to War 1922-1939* (London: Bloomsbury, 1991), 103.

82. William Manchester, *The Last Lion: Winston Spencer Churchill*, Vol. 2, *Alone 1932-1940* (Boston: Little Brown, 1988), 141.

83. Ibid., 141-42. Werner von Blomberg (1878-1946). Commander in Chief of the German Army, 1935-38. An advocate of a cautious German expansion, he was forced to resign on the eve of the Anschluss. Detained to testify at Nuremberg, he died of cancer.

84. Churchill, *Gathering Storm,* 175-76.

85. Kurt von Schuschnigg (1897-1977). Head of the semi-fascist Fatherland Front from 1933, he succeeded Dollfuss as Austrian Chancellor, 1934. Imprisoned by Hitler after the Anschluss, he was liberated in 1945 and emigrated to the U.S. in 1948, becoming a political science professor.

86. See for example David Hindley-Smith, who wrote Churchill from Vienna on 18 March 1938, saying the Viennese were "in despair." Churchill forwarded this to Geoffrey Dawson, editor of *The Times,* who demurred, telling Churchill of "the extraordinarily complete emotional surrender of the Austrians....There is no doubt, I think, that the impression of jubilation was overwhelming." CHUR 2/328, in Gilbert, *WSC,* Doc. Vol. 13, 949

87. Unity Mitford to Churchill, 5 March 1938. CHUR 2/328, ibid., 924-35. Mitford (1914-48) led a sorry life in Berlin as a Hitler sycophant, attempting suicide when Britain declared war on Germany in 1939; invalided back to Britain, she never came to terms with the Führer's downfall and died aged only 34.

88. Churchill, "The Annexation of Austria," House of Commons, 14 March 1948, *CS* VI 5925.

89. Ibid., 5926.

90. Ibid., 5927.

91. Churchill, "The Austrian Eye-Opener," *Evening Standard,* 18 March 1938.

92. Neville Chamberlain to his sister, , 20 March 1938, in Keith Feiling, *The Life of Neville Chamberlain* (London: Macmillan, 1946), 348. Gilbert, *Prophet of Truth,* 923.

93. Churchill, *Gathering Storm,* 214.

94. Ibid.

95. Bryan Perrett, *German Light Panzers* (London: Osprey, 1983), 35–37.

96. Alexander N. Lassner, "The Invasion of Austria in March 1938: Blitzkrieg or Pfusch?" in Günter Bishof & Anton Pelinka, eds., *Contemporary Austrian Studies*, Piscataway, N.J.: Transaction Publications, 2000, 447-87, quoted on http://www.panzercentral.com/forum/viewtopic.php?f=93&t=45354.

97. Churchill, *Gathering Storm,* 210-11. Werner von Fritsch (1880-1939). Member of the German High Command, dismissed with von Blomberg by Hitler before the Anschluss. He was killed during the invasion of Poland in 1939.

98. Hermann Goering to Czech Ambassador Dr. Voytech Mastny, Berlin, 11 March 1938 in David Faber, *Munich 1938* (New York: Simon & Schuster, 2009), 137.

Chapter 5

99. Churchill, "The Threat to Czechoslovakia," House of Commons, 24 March 1938, in *CS* VI 5941-43. Hansard vol. 333 cc1399-514, 1447-1451.

100. Churchill, *Gathering Storm*, 214.

101. Wilhelm Keitel (1882-1946). General 1937, Field Marshal 1940. Wehrmacht Chief of Staff and Minister of War 1938-45, Sudetenland Military Governor 1938. Keitel convinced Hitler to appoint his friend Walther von Brautisch as Commander-in-Chief of the Wehrmacht. He was hanged at Nuremberg.

102. Hitler to Keitel, 18 June 1938, in Gilbert, *WSC,* Biographic Volume 5, 954; see also www.battleofbritain1940.net (accessed 9 February 2015).

103. John H. Waller, *The Unseen War in Europe* (London: I.B. Taurus, 1996), 58.

104. Williamson Murray, "Munich and Its Alternative: The Case for Resistance," *Finest Hour* 152, Spring 2014, 17. For more details see Murray, *The Change in the European Balance of Power 1938-1939: The Path to Ruin* (Princeton, N.J.: Princeton University Press, 1984), chapters 6-8.

105. Ibid., 17-18.

106. Ibid., 18.

107. Ibid.

108. National Archives and Records Service Microfilm T-1022/3048/PG33272, Reichsverteidigungsausschuss, 15 December 1938.

109. Murray, "Munich and Its Alternative," 17.

110. Churchill, *Gathering Storm*, 243.

111. Ibid., 245-46.

112. Patricia Meehan, *The Unnecessary War: Whitehall and the German Resistance to Hitler* (London: Sinclair-Stevenson, 1992), 178.

113. William L. Shirer, *Berlin Diary* (New York: Knopf, 1941), 142-43.

114. Gilbert, *WSC* V, 987.

115. See Michael McMenamin, "Regime Change, 1938," *Finest Hour* 162, Spring 2014, 22-27.

116. Ibid.

117. Terry Parssinen, *The Oster Conspiracy of 1938: The Unknown Story of the Military Plot to Kill Hitler and Avert World War II* (New York: Harper Collins, 2003), 133-34. Meehan, *Unnecessary War*, 150.

118. Andrew Roberts, *The Holy Fox: Biography of Lord Halifax* (London: Weidenfeld & Nicolson, 1991), 108.

119. Hans Gisevius, *To the Bitter End: An Insider's Account of the Plot to Kill Hitler 1933-1945* (London: Cape, 1947), 296-304.

120. Gisevius, 326. McMenamin, 27.

121. Churchill, *Gathering Storm,* 244

122. Churchill, House of Commons, 5 October 1938, in Langworth, *CIHOW,* 258.

123. Murray, 17. Chris Bishop, *Encyclopedia of Weapons of World War II* (New York: Sterling, 2002), 128.

Chapter 6

124. J. Noakes & G. Pridham, eds., *Nazism 1919-1945*, Vol. 3, *Foreign Policy, War and Racial Extermination* (Exeter: University of Exeter Press, 2001), 119.

125. Ivan Mikhailovich Maisky (1884-1975). A half-Jewish Menshevik, he was exiled to Siberia by the Czar to Siberia, escaped, took an economics degree in Germany and lived in London 1912-17. Returning to Russia during the revolution, he became a Bolshevik. Soviet Ambassador to Britain, 1932-43, Deputy Foreign Minister, 1943-45. Imprisoned following an anti-Jewish purge 1949-53.

126. Donald Cameron Watt, "Churchill and Appeasement" in Blake, Robert and Louis, Wm. Roger. *Churchill: A Major New Assessment of His Life in Peace and War* (Oxford: Oxford University Press, 1993), 205.

127. Maisky to Churchill, 15 February and 31 March 1936, Churchill Papers (CHAR 2/251/53, CHAR 2/252). "Soviet envoy's book reveals missed opportunities to pre-empt Hitler's attack on the Soviet Union," *The*

Independent, London, 14 September 2015, online edition, http://ind.pn/1ib3soC, accessed 15 September 2015.

128. Gilbert, *WSC*, Doc. Vol. 13, 403; Churchill to Maisky, 14 November 1936, Churchill Papers (CHAR 2/260/93). Gilbert, WSC, Doc. Vol. 13, 410 n.1.

129. David Irving, *Churchill's War* (Bullsbrook, Australia: Veritas, 1987), 101. Though citations in this work are sometimes questionable, the quote is quite consistent with Churchill's attitude toward reaching an understanding with the Soviets. See note 135.

130. Manchester, *Last Lion,* II 452.

131. Churchill, *Gathering Storm,* 213.

132. Maisky to Churchill, Memorandum of 4 October 1938 (CHAR 9/130), in Gilbert, *WSC,* Doc. Vol. 13, 1201.

133. Churchill, *Gathering Storm,* 271.

134. R.A.C. Parker, *Chamberlain and Appeasement: British Policy and the Coming of the Second World War* (London: Palgrave Macmillan, 1993), 216-17.

135. Harold Nicolson: diary, 3 April 1939 (Nicolson Papers), in Gilbert, *WSC,* Document Vol. 13, 1429.

136. Churchill to John Colville, Chequers, 21 June 1941 in Langworth, *CIHOW,* 276.

137. Richard Lamb, *The Drift to War 1922-1939* (London: W.H. Allen, 1989), 300-01.

138. Manchester, *Last Lion,* Vol. 2, *Alone,* 452. Maxim Maximovich Litvinoff (1876-1951). Soviet Foreign Minister 1930-39, Ambassador to Washington 1941-43, Deputy Foreign Minister 1943-46. A Jew with an English wife, he lived many years in London. He took an accommodating line toward the Anglo-French, which abruptly ended when he was replaced by Molotov in May 1939.

139. Parker, *Chamberlain and Appeasement*, 228-29, 233.

140. Ibid., 227. Vyacheslav Mikhailovich Molotov (1890-1986). Minister of Foreign Affairs 1939-49, 1953-56, a hard-line Stalin protégé. Churchill wrote: "I have never seen a human being who more perfectly represented the modern conception of a robot....In the conduct of foreign affairs, Mazarin, Talleyrand, Metternich, would welcome him to their company, if there be another world to which Bolsheviks allow themselves to go." (*Gathering Storm*, 288-89). *The Independent*, 14 September 2015 (note 124).

141. Churchill, "The First Month of War," broadcast, London, 1 October 1939 in *CS* VI 6161; *Gathering Storm*, 286-87.

142. Earl of Birkenhead, *The Life of Lord Halifax* (London: Hamish Hamilton, 1965), 440.

143. Parker, *Chamberlain and Appeasement*, 232. For Litvinov's suggestion that Romania would allow passage of Soviet forces under League aegis, see Churchill's note to Halifax, 2 September 1938 (Foreign Office Papers 800/3222) in Gilbert, Doc. Vol. 13, 1137.

144. Charmley, *Lost Peace*, 189.

145. Parker, *Chamberlain and Appeasement*, 244-45.

146. Anthony Eden, *The Reckoning*, 75-76.

147. John W. Wheeler-Bennett, *Munich: Prologue to Tragedy* (New York: Duell, Sloan & Pearce, 1948), 388.

148. Reviewing *The Gathering Storm*, Walter Hall incorrectly claimed that Churchill resisted a Soviet alliance until 1938 (*Journal of Modern History*, XXI [1949], 358), but omitted to note that the Soviets did not propose a triple alliance until the 1938 Anschluss.

149. See for example Churchill's memo of his July 1938 conversation with Herr Foerster, Gauleiter of Danzig, and July-September correspondence with Halifax on Russia defending the Czechs via Romania in Gilbert, *WSC,* Doc. vol. 13, 1100-03, 1137-38.

150. See Powers, "Winston Churchill's Parliamentary Commentary," 182.

Chapter 7

151. See for example Bob Ruggenberg, "Why America Should Have Stayed Out," *The Heritage of the Great War,* http:// xrl.us/2s8z.

152. See Winston S. Churchill, *The World Crisis,* vol. III, part 1 *1916-1918* (London: Thornton Butterworth, 1927), 226-27.

153. Ibid., 214.

154. *National Enquirer,* http://bit.ly/juAt0j, accessed November 2013.

155. John Roy Carlson, *Under Cover: My Four Years in the Nazi Underworld of America* (New York: Dutton, 1943), 246.

156. Enquirer/Star Group, Inc. Company History, www.fundinguniverse.com, accessed November 2013.

157. Churchill Private Office notes, Chartwell Papers (hereinafter "CHAR"), Churchill Archives Centre, CHAR 2/383/44-46.

158. Winston S. Churchill, "The Truth About War Debts," *Answers,* 17 March 1934, reprinted in *The Collected Essays of Sir Winston Churchill,* 4 vols. (London: Library of Imperial History, 1975) II 313-15.

159. William Griffin, "When Churchill Said Keep Out!" (reprint of the 1936 *Enquirer* article) *Scribner's Commentator,* February 1941, pp 25-28.

160. William N. Stokes, Jr. to Senator Robert R. Reynolds, enclosed in Stokes's letter to Churchill, 22 July 1939, CHAR 2/383/12. The inference is that this allegation surfaced in summer 1939. Reynolds remained isolationist through 1941, when the Roosevelt Administration arranged for him to be shuffled aside as North Carolina senator.

161. Stokes to Churchill, 27 September 1939, CHAR 2/383/12.

162. Alan C. Collins to Churchill, 19 September 1939, CHAR 2/383/1. Churchill Archives cuttings file, CHAR 2/383/26.

163. Churchill to J. Arthur Levy, 1 November 1939 CHAR 2/383/25-26.

164. *The New York Times*, Thursday, 22 October 1942 and *Times* archives researched by Michael McMenamin.

165. Winston S. Churchill, "Great Events of Our Time," Part III, "The Decisive Factor in the Allied Victory," *News of the World*, London, 13 June 1937, in *The Collected Essays* IV 371-72.

166. Churchill, *Gathering Storm*, 3-15.

167. See for example Jonathan Petropoulos, *Royals and the Reich* (Oxford University Press, 2006), 170 et. seq. and Alan Palmer, *The Kaiser: Warlord of the Second Reich* (New York: Scribner, 1978), 226.

168. Churchill, "The Truth About War Debts," 313.

169. Churchill to James Roosevelt, Chartwell, 8 October 1938, in Kay Halle, *Irrepressible Churchill* (Cleveland: World, 1966), 7-8.

170. Churchill, "Election Address," Woodford, in *CS* VI 5687.

171. Roosevelt's "Quarantine Speech," 5 October

1937, at
http://millercenter.org/president/fdroosevelt/speeches/spee
ch-3310, accessed March 2015.

172. Churchill, "Foreign Affairs," Conservative Party
Conference, Scarborough, 7 October 1937, in *CS* VI 5895.

173. Churchill, Constituency Meeting, Waltham
Abbey, 26 October 1937, in *CS* VI 5898.

174. Churchill, "Anglo-American Unity," Harvard, 6
September 1943, in Langworth, *CIHOW,* 119.

175. Chamberlain to his sister in William Rock,
Chamberlain and Roosevelt (Columbus: Ohio State
University Press, 1988) 54

176. Gilbert, *WSC,* Document Volume 13, 902, n.2.
Horace John Wilson (1882-1972). Civil servant, seconded
to the Treasury for special service with Stanley Baldwin,
1935-37 and with Neville Chamberlain, 1937-40 (when he
had a room at 10 Downing Street). Permanent Secretary to
the Treasury and Head of the Civil Service, 1939-42.

177. Ibid., Horace Wilson to P.J. Grigg, 31 January
1938.

178. Churchill, *Gathering Storm,* 199.

179. Roosevelt to Churchill, 11 September 1939,
message R-1x, in Warren F. Kimball, ed., *Roosevelt and
Churchill: The Complete Correspondence*, 3 vols.
(Princeton: Princeton University Press, 1984), I 24. While
at the Admiralty, Churchill sent no messages of political or
strategic substance. They did speak on the telephone more
than once, but Churchill tactfully did not mention this in
his memoirs.

180. Churchill, *Gathering Storm,* 345.

181. Churchill, "Anglo-American Unity," Harvard
University, 6 September 1943, in Langworth, *CIHIOW*,
21-22, 134.

Chapter 8

182. Churchill, *Gathering Storm,* 251.

183. Williamson Murray, "Munich and Its Alternative," *Finest Hour* 162, Spring 2014, 16.

184. Parker, *Chamberlain and Appeasement,* 272.

185. Churchill, "Defence," Speech to the New Commonwealth Society, Dorchester Hotel, London, 25 November 1936, *CS* VI 5815.

186. Churchill, *Gathering Storm,* vii.

187. Baldwin in Hansard (Parliamentary Debates), 12 November 1936, 317: 1144-45. The index entry, "confesses to putting party before country," is in *The Gathering Storm,* 615.

188. Churchill to Archibald Boyd-Carpenter, 13 November 1936, in Gilbert, *WSC,* Doc. Vol. 13, 405.

189. Churchill, *Gathering Storm,* 169-70.

190. See for example Middlemas & Barnes, *Baldwin,* 971, and David Reynolds, *In Command of History: Churchill Fighting and Writing the Second World War* (London: Allen Lane, 2004), 95-96.

191. Ibid., 169; Churchill, *Arms and the Covenant,* 385-86.

192. Baldwin in Hansard, 317: 1145-46.

193. Churchill in Hansard, 317: 1104-05.

194. Churchill, House of Commons, 20 July 1936, in Langworth, *CIHOW,* 493.

195. "Britain's Deficiencies in Aircraft Manufacture," 28 April 1938, in Winston S. Churchill, *Step by Step* (London: Thornton Butterworth, 1939), 226.

196. Churchill, "The Annexation of Austria," House of Commons, 14 March 1938, in *CS* VI 5924.

197. Churchill, *Gathering Storm,* 214.

198. Andrew Roberts, *The Holy Fox* (London: Weidenfeld & Nicolson, 1991) 112-22; John Charmley, *Churchill: The End of Glory* (New York: Harcourt Brace, 1993), 347. Roberts notes that by "great mass of public opinion," Halifax "really meant his own opinion, together with that of whichever friends he had spoken to and newspapers he had read."

199. Winston S. Churchill, interview by Kingsley Martin, editor, *The New Statesman,* 7 January 1939, republished 7 January 2014, http://bit.ly/19PDVfN.

200. William L. Shirer, *Berlin Diary: The Journal of a Foreign Correspondent, 1934-1941* (New York: Taylor & Francis, 2002, reprint), 142-43. Hjalmar Schacht, *Account Settled* (London: Weidenfeld & Nicolson, 1949), 124.

201. McMenamin, "Regime Change, 1938," *Finest Hour* 162, 23.

202. Churchill, *Gathering Storm,* 251.

203. Parker, *Chamberlain and Appeasement,* 271.

204. Ibid.

205. Churchill, *Gathering Storm,* 196.

206. Patricia Meehan, *The Unnecessary War: Whitehall and the German Resistance to Hitler* (London: Sinclair-Stevenson, 1992), 178.

207. Churchill, House of Commons, 12 November 1940, in Langworth, *CIHOW,* 53.

208. Churchill, broadcast to America, 16 October 1938, in Gilbert, *WSC,* Doc. Vol. 13, 1217.

About the Author

Richard M. Langworth began his Churchill work in 1968 when he organized the Churchill Study Unit and its journal, *Finest Hour*. The Study Unit later became the International Churchill Society and finally the Churchill Centre, devoted to all aspects of Churchill's life. Mr. Langworth served as its president (1996-2000), board chairman (2000-06) and editor of *Finest Hour* (1982-2014). In November 2014, Mr. Langworth was appointed senior fellow for Hillsdale College's Churchill Project.

In 1998, Richard Langworth was appointed a Commander of the Most Excellent Order of the British Empire by Her Majesty The Queen "for services to Anglo-American understanding and the memory of Sir Winston Churchill."

Mr. Langworth published the first American edition of Churchill's *India*, is the author of *A Connoisseur's Guide to the Books of Sir Winston Churchill*, and is the editor of *Churchill by Himself, The Definitive Wit of Winston Churchill, The Patriot's Churchill, All Will Be Well: Good Advice from Winston Churchill, Churchill in His Own Words*, and *Churchill and the Avoidable War*. His next book is *Winston Churchill, Urban Myths and the Truth: An Antidote to Red Herrings, Tall Tales, Fables and Nonsense*.

For more information visit richardlangworth.com or email the author at caw-rml@sneakemail.com.

About The Churchill Project

Hillsdale College has launched the Churchill Project to propagate a right understanding of Churchill's record, and to "teach statesmanship" through its distinguished academic resources at all levels from undergraduate to online education programs.

Since 2006, Hillsdale College Press has been the publisher of *Winston S. Churchill,* the official biography, including its eight biographic and nineteen document volumes produced through 2016. The Churchill Project will complete the remaining volumes of *The Churchill Documents,* bringing to over thirty volumes what is already the longest biography in history.

The Churchill Project is also the archive for the papers of Sir Martin Gilbert, Churchill's official biographer from 1968 to 2012. And it will promote Churchill scholarship through national conferences, scholarships, online courses, and an endowed faculty chair. Through these endeavours, Hillsdale College will establish itself at the forefront of Churchill research, scholarship, and analysis.

For more information please visit The Churchill Project website, winstonchurchill.hillsdale.edu, where you may subscribe for frequent updates of articles and videos.

Made in the USA
Charleston, SC
06 November 2015